Endorsements

April's storytelling ability truly draws the reader in. It's like we are right there with her watching it all happen. Equally magnetic are her metaphors surrounding light, darkness, and the shame shadow. Out of Darkness is sure to inspire many to come out of darkness and choose the light. Realizing our power to choose is perhaps the most healing piece of it all.

—Audrey May Prosper,
Activist and Creator of Your Thrive Tribe

April Tribe Giauque has offered a must-read book for anyone whose life journey and circumstances have propelled them into a place of darkness. Drawing us in with her personal examples and expert storytelling, while beautifully contrasting lightness and darkness, she reminds us over and over again that we have a choice.

—Aleta Norris,
Best-selling author of *Women Who Spark.*

It's time to stop hiding in the darkness and live in the light. We all have elements of both hiding inside of us, but the choice is ours to decide which path we take. April uses vivid stories to put you on the path to healing and teaches you how not to let shame or fear stop you from shining bright.

—Chellie Phillips,
Award Winning Author of *When in Doubt, Delete It.*

Out of Darkness

Find, Fuel, and Live in Your Light

By
April Tribe Giauque

Paperback: 978-1-64746-135-5
Hardback: 978-1-64746-136-2
Ebook: 978-1-64746-137-9

(LCCN): 2020901906

Dedication

To my husband, family and to everyone who has heard the phrase, "you are not enough" that has come from somewhere deep within. This is your first step towards leaving that Darkness and walking into your Light!

Table of Contents

Section 3: Recovering, Reflecting & Resting

Section 4: Finding, Fueling, and Amplifying Your Light

Introduction

On October 29, 1941, at Harrow School in England, Winston Churchill delivered his famous "Never give up speech." Here is the quote from the speech, "Never give in. Never give in. Never, never, never—in nothing, great or small, large or petty—never give in, except to convictions of honour and good sense. Never yield to force. Never yield to the apparently overwhelming might of the enemy".

He went on to say, "Do not let us speak of darker days: let us speak rather of sterner days. These are not dark days; these are great days—the greatest days our country has ever lived; and we must all thank God that we have been allowed, each of us according to our stations, to play a part in making these days memorable in the history of our race."

During that time, the Blitz was raging and nightly, the people of London were being bombed by German forces. There was nothing to stop them but for the small Royal Air Force and the will of the people. It seemed insurmountable and hopeless. How could Winston Churchill claim that they were the "greatest days our country has ever lived?" Because through adversity they became stronger. Through the trials, the hardships, and even the deaths, they learned what it took to defeat the enemy. They discovered the internal will to find hope and light within each individual and then collectively come together to scorch a pathway through the enemy's darkness.

Light and darkness. The opposing forces are not new. They are as old as life itself. The forces of light and darkness both live within you. This is a very personal battle that can rage inside our hearts, our minds, and our souls. We are faced with a lifetime of battling the enemies of negativity, hate, degrading words, of passive-aggressiveness, and worse in our head.

I feel called to share my experiences of how I battled my enemy. I feel called to help you *Out of Darkness*. Through this book, I will empower you to find your light. It is a journey of discovering your light out of Comfort Cages through Learning Zones and allowing you to be at your most vulnerable self. But it is the only way to discover the true power of your light, how to fuel it and amplify it so that you can live in your light!

In order to do that fully, you must understand the darkness of your enemy, the Shame Shadow©. I teach you how to identify him, *call him out,* and empower you with skills to know how to stay in your light and out of the darkness. Just like the blitz, we have to find a way to not just survive this battle, but to defend ourselves and win!

Please NEVER give in to it. Be strong as England of old. Draw on the strength of your light as the enemy beats upon your mind and stand firm. These are GREAT days! The GREATEST that you and the world have ever seen. Remember that everything has its opposite. So as dark and evil happen in life, hope and LIGHT are stronger and will overcome—if we *Never, Never, Never, Never give in!*

SECTION 1

Eternal Truth

CHAPTER 1

Opposition in All things

Success is not measured by what you accomplish, but by the opposition you have encountered, and the courage with which you have maintained the struggle against overwhelming odds.—Orisen Swett Marden

"For it must needs be, that there is an opposition in all things. If not so, my firstborn in the wilderness, righteousness could not be brought to pass, neither wickedness, neither holiness nor misery, neither good nor bad. Wherefore, all things must needs be a compound in one; wherefore, if it should be one body it must needs remain as dead, having no life neither death, nor corruption nor incorruption, happiness nor misery, neither sense nor insensibility" (2 Nephi 2:11).

Light/dark, health/sickness, pain/pleasure, misery/joy, faith/fear, force/freedom, life/death. What are these? They are opposites. Opposites are found everywhere. Do you believe that? Do you believe that because of opposition we will need to make choices? What happens if you can't make choices and you are forced to do something. Do you like it?

You picked up this book and started reading it. No one forced you to do that. You made a choice. Maybe curiosity urges you to find out things and try out different things and you have the freedom to do that. What I'm talking about here is found in all things. Think of science in particular physics. Newton's third law is: "For every action, there is an **equal** and **opposite reaction**." The statement means that in every interaction, there is a pair of forces acting on the two interacting objects. The size of the forces on the first object **equals** the size of the force on the second object.

As a woman of faith, I believe that the foundation of the plan of our Heavenly Father is to have agency—this opportunity to make a choice. Whether you believe this or not, just hear me out for the next few paragraphs. I believe and know that Heavenly Father will force no man to heaven. He desires us to have agency and make that choice between our divine nature and the natural man.

In fact, even before we were born on earth, I believe that we were spiritually created in heaven by our Heavenly Father and Heavenly Mother. That we were all a family in Heaven with Him. While we loved our life there, we had progressed as far as we could, and it was time to make a choice. A plan was presented— one that allowed us to have agency and make a choice to come to earth have opposition in all things and see what we will pick in order to return Home to Heaven (agency). There was another plan presented that guaranteed not losing one person and ALL returning to Heaven (force).

We were all there listening to what was happening and finally there came a time where we had to make a choice, our first one. Would we follow the plan of agency or the plan of force? He hopes that we make choices that lead us back to

Him. Our test here is to prove ourselves to see if we can make it back. What a hero's journey right? Look at all the choices that it gives us.

Two opposites are Divine Nature/Natural Man

Divine Nature: coming from the Lord, from Heaven, from a place of intense love. "All human beings—male and female— are created in the image of God. Each is a beloved spirit son or daughter of heavenly parents and, as such, each has a divine nature and destiny." ("The Family: A Proclamation to the World," *Ensign,* Nov. 2010, 129). We all have a *piece of Heaven with us* and we all are born with the *Light of Christ* inside us. That light of Christ is our moral compass—the way that we can tell right from wrong, light from darkness, love or the lack of it.

Natural Man: this is the part of us that sometimes likes to be mischievous. The natural man will push back on the truth just to see what will happen. In short, the natural man is rebellion. The natural man is a person who *chooses* to be influenced by the passions, desires, appetites, and "senses of the flesh" rather than by the promptings of the Holy Spirit. When we are only thinking in our natural man, we can comprehend physical things but not spiritual things. and Peter says, "The natural man receiveth not the things of the Spirit." (1 Cor. 2:14).

Right there, out of the gate, is the definition and smack down of who we are. We are divine creatures who have natural man tendencies. Wow! What opposites! Divine nature and the natural man. The opposition here is very striking.

For the purposes of this book I will call the divine nature Light, and the natural man is Darkness! We have both light and dark within us. The famous quote by the character Sirius Black from JK Rowling is "We've all got both light and dark inside us. What matters is the part we choose to act on. That's who we really are." (Harry Potter, Order of the Phoenix). In order to know the good from the bad, we need to understand that there is opposition in *all* things. Bottomline we all have a choice!

The real question is: why do we follow, give in to, and are tempted by the natural man? Answer? It is so that we have the opportunity to make a choice. The agency to choose the natural man or choose to act with our Divine Nature. What powerful and beautiful freedom! But wait, some of you might want to ask, why can't we just choose the right and stick to the one way—even by a little force?

Think about your life as you were growing up, when you had the option of choices that were given to you; did you feel empowered, happier, and feel like you were in control? Choices allow for this. If we have already established that there is "opposition in all things" and we want to have choices, then the idea of forcing someone to do something becomes an infringement on that right.

As a woman of faith, I believe that the foundation of the plan of our Heavenly Father is to have agency—this opportunity to make a choice. Whether you believe this or not, just hear me out for the next few paragraphs. I believe and know that Heavenly Father will force no man to heaven. He desires us to have agency and make that choice between our divine nature and the natural man.

In fact, even before we were born on earth, I believe that we were spiritually created in heaven by our Heavenly Father and Heavenly Mother. That we were all a family in heaven with Him, and so we are all He wants. He wants us to choose Him because we have found Him, love Him, and want to serve Him. This is a choice to do those things or to serve the destroyer. Mathew 6: 24 states, "No man can serve two masters: for either he will hate the one and love the other; or else he will hold to the one and despise the other. Ye cannot serve God and mammon."

Since we have agency, we can choose which "team" we want to be on. But the decision is going to be put on a battlefield every day. You'll find out what you are made of as you make these decisions. Here is a secret. Wouldn't you like to know the rules of the game— who's side you belong to—even who you are? Yes? Then you are in the right place!

I've heard it said that the winning score is already up on the board. Meaning we already know which team is going to win (Good over Evil. God over Satan). We know who will win so why on earth do we spend our time switching teams? Jefferey R Holland said, "So we need young men [and young women] already on the team to *stay* on it and stop dribbling out of bounds just when we need you to get in the game and play your hearts out!" (General Conference Oct 2011 We are All Enlisted).

So why do we get confused and "dribble" out of bounds? Why do we fall and get out of bounds; even join the losing team for a while? Because we have the agency to do so. The Lord will force no man to heaven, but He will allow us to feel good and bad, - joyful and depressed, pleasure and pain so that we can use those learning experiences as memories to not repeat them again. We have the agency to learn many of these lessons early or late in life, but nonetheless, we will learn them.

The opposition of faith and fear play a huge component to see on which team we are going to stay. The Lord's team plays with faith and Satan's team plays with fear!

Faith as a child is so simple. Faith as a child is just doing and acting without questioning anything. It is living life to the fullest and finding joy. The power of faith causes action; and in that act of believing in something, that is when you exercise your faith by taking action. You take action even though you have no proof or evidence but a hope or a belief. Once you decide to take action based on the hope/belief then you have stepped into faith. Faith equals action towards that hope/belief/light!

Fear. What is it? "An unpleasant emotion caused by the threat of danger, pain, or harm to oneself rationally or irrationally" (Webster Dictionary). Fear dispels faith. It is the opposite of faith. In fear resides all the negative emotions, the "real" terror, or the threat.

Let's start with faith. My faith, in knowing that my Heavenly Father is real and is watching over me from Heaven has been there my whole life. I knew that Heavenly Father listens to my prayers and loves me. It has been demonstrated time and time again because He answered my prayers. I had a sense of communication with Him long before I really understood how to pray. I felt that He was just with me in my heart and that He was always listening to me.

I felt a warmth within me that felt like pure light especially when I would pray. Through that light, my mind would come alive with thoughts that gave me joy and energy. I could feel a sense of communication through His light. He was like a clarifying thought and a warm feeling in my head and heart. When I saw the truth, I instantly had goosebumps on my legs and a giggle in my heart. It was similar to a physical voice but with more intensity and clarity. I just knew that He was there for me as I knew that the sun would rise every morning. I knew that He would never forsake me but be there always for me.

Once when I was about age four, I was in my room, and I couldn't remember where I placed my favorite teddy bear, "Papi-bear." I suddenly couldn't find it. My heart was instantly engaged in a prayer asking for help to find it. I searched under my bed, under my dresser, and in my toys. Hot tears were falling on my cheeks and I was about to give up when I saw the bear out of the corner of my eye stuck between my bed rail and my sheets. I ran, pulled it out, and thanked my Heavenly Father for helping me. I had the sweetest feeling of love burst in my little heart that told me my Heavenly Father was always listening to me.

The simple story of a child can be easily discounted or "eye-rolled" away, but really look at it. At four years of age and without any fear/doubt (I had not learned how to listen to that voice) I took **action**. Faith is action. I was in need (help to find the bear), and so I asked (said my prayer), and I took action (actively searching for the bear). Result? Bear found (all credit goes to Heavenly Father for listening to me and helping me) and prayers of gratitude rise upward. Do we have that kind of child-like faith? Are we willing to submit and ask for help? Or as we grow up do we also grow apart from that faith like action— the willingness to submit our will to His and take action? What stops us? Doubt and fear? (More on that in just a bit).

Doubts Can be Small...But So Destructive

When I think about Light I think about our self-worth. **Self-worth** is the opinion you **have** about yourself and the **value** you place on yourself. What is Lack? Lack is the void of light—the disorienting darkness of **self-doubt.** Doubt is very powerful, and it can cause great harm to our self-worth if we stay the darkness of it. Yet if we turn ourselves towards the light then there is no more darkness. The opposition in all things returns. We have this so that we can make choices, and hopefully, we are choosing light over the darkness.

Doubts to Dumb

I could hear the booming voice of my teacher. "It's time for spelling. We are going to play a game called stand and spell." My stomach suddenly flipped and fluttered inside. I knew this game. My first-grader heart was skipping around in my chest like a caged bird. I hated spelling especially out loud and in front of my peers. Waiting for my name to be called was giving me a serious case of the butterflies!

My eyes scanned across the classroom. Soon it would be my turn to spell a word from the list. One more then it would be me! Oh no! I hated stand and spell. The game in school that showed my classmates one more of my flaws. Talk about being totally exposed and vulnerable. I knew that this game would reveal all that I lacked.

"April," came the teacher's voice. "Spell sick." What?? I thought? Sick? This was a word I actually knew! I could not believe my luck. I smiled, stood up, took a full breath and said the letters loud and proud, "C-i-ick. Sick!" Giggles rang out in the classroom and my teacher's eye peered over her glasses. Then a tone of disgust she said, "Sit down!"

I felt my knees buckle, which forced me into my chair. My mind was racing. C-i- ick, C-i-ick. That is how you spelled it. I kept saying over and over in my mind, *that's how my dad spells it, my grandpa spells it, and how my mom spells it!*' I could not believe what happened. I looked around at a few faces that were smirking and laughing and felt my pink flush up, splotching my face. I was still in disbelief. I opened up the speller to the spelling list and there in black and white was the word "sick" s-i-c-k. I had no words other than to feel so betrayed by my family.

Suddenly a thought popped. Your family must know something you don't. Hum...can you trust them? Then something else popped into my head that day to confirm in my mind one word *you must be dumb.* I knew it had to be true, especially when it came to spelling. I would fight with the letters to stay in their place and not jump all over the page. I would go over and over the words and only come up with a beginning letter and the ending letter but everything else in the middle was up for grabs. See, I am dumb! And I started believing it. That was my first real memory of doubt. It was a gut-puncher and my first experience filling my mind with lack, which pushed out the light.

Opposition happens in all things throughout life. Why? It is how we are to learn. Why? So that we can understand the bitter from the sweet, the lows and the highs, and the good from the evil and so forth. In the Bible, conflict between good and evil is throughout the book (whether you believe in the Bible or not this principle is found there).

One example is Genesis 2:9, "And out of the ground made the Lord God to grow every tree that is pleasant to the sight, and good for food; the tree of life also in the midst of the garden, and the tree of knowledge of good and evil." Tree of life … and the tree of knowledge of good and evil. Since I knew my Heavenly Father was there for me, I was next going to have to learn about Satan just like Adam and Eve did. After experiencing doubt, an opportunity to experience fear was next.

I was about eight years old at the time when I was asked to go to a birthday party. I didn't really know what to expect or what to think other than I wanted to be with the big kids. I was going to be with the twelve-year old girls. I was going to be "cool."

The Birthday Party

I stepped out of the bathroom and toward the giggles and low whispering of the girl in the TV den. I quietly peeked into the room, which was dim with just a few candles to give off their feeble light. Nine girls were huddled around a coffee table, all focused with sickening fascination to a board with letters printed on it. *What was that thing*, I wondered to myself? *Why was the movie off? Why were we going to have some cake and ice cream?* I didn't want to say anything and look like the baby so I just stood in the back waiting to see what would happen.

The candles flickering and the girls all focused and giggling gave me a sense that they all knew something I didn't. Then someone asked the first question. Suddenly I could feel my skin prickle, giving me the chills. Then there was a scraping sound of the finder sliding along the board racing towards a letter, then another, and another, until her question was answered with a word. Another question was asked, and the same sliding occurred and "Oh's" and "ah's" from girls echoed out. I broke from my stare with the board and forced myself to look around the room. I felt a cold sweep over me and enter into the room.

Finally, another question was asked, but with this came a change that entered into the room. It was not a feeling of light, but I felt my spirit darken with that coldness. I could hear a continuation of their questions and the scraping of the strangely shaped disk against the surface of the board. I did my best not to watch it slide all around the letters. The coldness of the room was followed by a deeper feeling of darkness. The physical light in the room was dim but this feeling seemed to darken it even more. The scraping sound of the disk, the cold, the dark feeling and finally a word was spelled which caused us all to scream out!

I was struck with terror and fear, and for the first time in my life, I felt a hole, a black hole, and lack of light. My home had never had anything like this. My home was filled with love and light, and not this unwelcomed dark feeling. I could not understand it. I my legs were filled with energy and they turned to break out of the darkness of the room. I ran to get my things. All I knew was that I had the feeling to get out.

I turned back up the hallway toward the front door. I could see the handle. I was almost there. I was still clutching my sleeping bag, pillow, and stuffed animal in my arms, and ran right into my friend, the birthday girl. My breath caught in my throat. I was not only looking at her, but at the entire party of girls all staring at me. My heart was pounding because I felt trapped. I wanted out. I did not want the darkness that was in that room; and now it felt like the entire house. I stepped aside to push through the group when she grabbed me by the arm. She said, "Don't be a baby."

That statement grounded me to the spot. Suddenly I could feel the eyes of nine twelve-year-old girls staring at my eight-year-old self, and again I was trapped. I did NOT want to be the baby. They looked at me with daring eyes and folded arms and scowling faces. I could feel the hot pink start creep up my neck and color my checks again. Even in the light of the candles I knew they could see me flush.

I was faced with a choice. What I call a "real choice" the one that counts. Again, from the eyes and the jeering, I looked at my friend to find some hope. But no. All I found was the same response—even anger and threatening eyes. I felt I would be hurt if I left, so I crumbled. I stayed at the party out of fear. My fear to please others overruled my feeling to flea and to get somewhere safe.

Over my lifetime, what I learned was that Satan snuffs out all light and hope. He destroys the truth. He lies; he mingles truth with lies in such a clever way that you are torn—con-flicted! Satan preys upon your emotions and twists them against the truth you thought you knew with absolution. Satan and his team of destroyers have sought to destroy my testimony of my Heavenly Father from a young age. Thus, my battle to understand between right and wrong had really begun.

CHAPTER 2

Let there be Light!

Give light and people will find a way. —Ella Baker

"And God said, 'Let there be light: and there was light."
Genesis 1:3

Individual Worth or Worthlessness

Time to switch gears and geek out a little bit. Let's look at this: For many years, lovers of science have said that humans are made of the same elements as the stars. And now after studying over 150,000 stars, the statement is actually true! "We are made of stardust!" "Humans and their galaxy have about 97 percent of the same kind of atoms and the elements of life appear to be more prevalent toward the galaxy's center." (Karl Tate)

According to - scientists the building blocks of life or the crucial elements for life on Earth, "can be abbreviated as CHNOPS: carbon, hydrogen, nitrogen, oxygen, phosphorus, and sulfur." Scientists have been searching for CHNOPS in the stars and, "for the first time, astronomers have cataloged the abundance of these elements in a huge sample of stars." (Elizabeth Howell Space.com contributor and writer).

How do the scientists know? Spectroscopy! To summarize, each element gives off an amount of energy or wavelength of light. Each wavelength or energy gives off an emission of this light. It is a unique color signature for the elements/atoms. Therefore, the stars each give off different colors depending on what - element it comes from. Astronomers measure the depth of the dark and bright patches in each star's light spectrum and since each emission signature is unique to each element, they can determine what it is made of. (Natural, World Physics).

After all that work, we now have scientific proof that we are made of the same elements as the stars! For me personally, I have always known this. We are made from light! This is what makes our self-worth, our individual worth, of such value! It is my soul. I don't call it self-esteem because esteem comes from man. Worth and value comes from our Creator. What happens when we believe and exercise our faith that we have this individual worth? And what happens when we don't believe it? You will discover that through the stories in the book as well as for yourself.

Individual Worth/ Worthlessness
Let's start with Individual Worth

Individual Worth is the sense of one's own value or **worth** as a person. Remember that this worth is our light! It is what helps us shine. How do we know what we are worth? Let's look back a chapter. If we are from a divine nature or from a creator, God, Heavenly Father whatever you believe that to be, then your worth of who you are individually is of infinite worth.

Your worth is equivalent to light! He has planted this light in our soul. The worth of souls is great light. We all have a light inside of us and that light is our self-worth.

Why is it that we see light in people's eyes? Have you ever looked into the eyes of a newborn baby? They have such we can see the light—that self-worth? They are innocent and full of love, light, and determination to live life. No matter what circumstances they have been born into they still bring that light from within them and they know who they belong to. After all, they just left His presence.

What happens as we grow up? What dims our light? Is it something that happens to you-? Is it what others say about you? Is it fear or worry? Maybe a combination of all three? Yes, it is a combination of all three and that is what I believe to be true.

Regardless, I want you all to know that you all have light within you! You all have a spark and flame; a source of energy that lights up your eyes! It is the light of Christ and it is our self-worth, self-love, and I say LIGHT! I want you to know that you can brighten your light no matter what you have been through in this lifetime: abuse, abandonment, anger, hurt, pain, death, loss, sorrow, divorce, disappointment, shame, loss of perfection, failures at home, work, or school. ANYTHING!

Your light, your worth—your identity, is crucial to know who you are, why you are here, and where you are going! That all comes back to LIGHT! In order to find this light, you need to believe that you have it inside of you no matter who or what circumstances might have dimmed it. You have your light as long as you have living breath.

Imagining Light

Round and round the toy record player would spin. I lifted up the needle and gently put it down on the spinning vinyl record. Instantly notes, words, stories, and music would fill the room, giving me a pallet in which to paint my world. My light was happy here. Safe here! My stage was a tiled countertop which rested upon the storage cabinets in the back room or the playroom. My feet would dance along the tiled countertops to the notes that leapt out of the speakers. My voice would sing the songs over and over again and again. This world of imagination would become so real to me with each retelling and singing of the stories, that I would be consumed in it for hours. This light was strengthening.

At times my feet were stilled—no music would be playing—but instead I would be reciting the scripts and dramatic roles of many different characters. I would learn how to warp and twist my feelings to match what they were acting out in the story. I could envision an entire world complete with color, sound, voice, and music. I would act and act to my audience of stuffed animals. I would use my hands to scribble - out a letter—a cry for help—and put it in a bottle so that someone would hear my message. I would look left, then right to make sure that I was alone, and then I would drop the bottle into the vast ocean of blue carpet that surrounded my tiled stage and I would hope someone would read my note as I played the part and character of someone else.

Playing alone was safe and a great way to learn how to create stories, start writing, and find my light. I was in the joy of my light when I would play like this. I would play for hours. I was alone but not alone. I was developing my light, my love, my ability to understand myself. I loved to play and pretend. I knew that I was deeply loved. This feeling was my baseline of love and light!

What happens when your baseline of love and light is then threatened? Remember in Chapter one we will have opposition in all things. I had experienced light and love, so it was time to experience the opposite of that.

Stuffed with Pain

Bum-thump, bum-thump, bum-thump, bum-thump came the feeling from my chest! My heart was racing. Was I really ready? My 7-year-old mind suddenly filled my backyard with a childhood scene from my imagination, and I had painted a scene unlike any game I had ever played before. Suddenly before me, the green grass changed to a torrent of water that had filled a river. The deep grey waters mixed with speed and with the air, causing whitecaps, frothy, foamy, bubbly crashing waves that churned down the river.

Sprays of water hit my face. The river was pounding on the shiplap siding on at the base of the little home. The noise of the raging waters and pounding waves was a deafening roar. I had mere moments before the water would strip the siding from the structure (the playhouse), and I would be taken with it. I had climbed up to the roof of the little structure and felt it shudder and moan with the power of the raging river slam it's flooding waters against it.

I had only one choice. I had to scale across the zipline to the large American sycamore tree. The structure shuddered again. This was it. I reached, pulling my ten fingers tightly around the grip of the zipline and launched myself into the air! My body felt like time had slowed to a crawl. I felt the slow-motion zip down the line with my feet dangling just inches above the grey and white raging waters, which sprayed me with their teasing grasp.

My left hand slipped, and I dangled by one arm as I zipped toward the tree in dramatic effect. The music and rage of the water filled my mind as the tree zoomed closer! I glanced behind me ever so slowly, and I heard the crashing, snapping, and gutting sound of the white shiplap structure splinter into thousands of toothpicks! I had leaped in the nick of time!

Timing was everything for the next hurdle, I must release my grasp from the zipline at the right forward propelling moment to maximize the flight of my body in order to land on the other side of the river. The energy from the zipline was perfect and I released my grip and flew into the air. I was stretched out and suspended in time or a moment. In that second the music, the rage of the river, the spot of grass on the other side of the river all came into focus and I hit the target with precision!

As soon as my feet connected back with the earth, the imagination of the game was over. The rage of the river dried up, the destruction of the structure had been rebuilt, and the dramatic music was off. My play adventure was over. The backyard looked like it always had: the grass, shrubbery was along the perimeter of the fenced yard, the white A-framed playhouse/shed combo was in the corner of the yard, the apple tree, and the grapevines where all there. The raging river of my imagination had never destroyed anything. It was time to go inside for a snack. Afterall, imagining the river, the destruction, and my heroic zipline and leap to safety made me thirsty.

I ran through the house to the kitchen to get a drink of water. Upon entering the kitchen, I saw a scene of horror that was burned into my heart. I entered into the kitchen with the mangled bodies of *my* stuffed animals dangled from nooses! Each one of my animal friends hung by ropes from the knobs of the kitchen cabinets. The stuffed animals had bags over their faces as they stiffly rotated in the air. My animals! My things! My world!

I could only focus on the sickening swinging of each of my stuffed friends. Who could have done such a terrible thing? In my shock and flash of hurt and anger, I reached and jumped and screamed trying to grab at my stuffed animals. But the stuffed animals were moved and pulled away from my grasp. My sisters kept them out of my hands while their laughter mocked my efforts.

I finally reached out for "Pandora" (my *Shirt Tales* panda) and grasped her. I grabbed a knife and started sawing her free from her rope. Once free, I dropped the knife and ran to my room and the mocking laughter seemed to follow me up the stairs. Then suddenly I heard a voice that was not from them but from a dark place, somewhere else say, "*unlovable.*" It pulled me up short in my crying and my breath caught. It was a dark voice and one that I would begin to hear inside my head over and over again as I grew up. It repeated, "*unlovable.*" That word seemed to cut deeper than the mocking laughter—it cut at my very being. I just cried and cried.

I think I must have fallen asleep from the emotional exhaustion of the afternoon because when I lifted my head the light was dim, like twilight. It was in that quiet light, in that quiet moment that I remembered praying and crying to my Heavenly Father and telling him that my heart was broken. Why did my sisters do that?

From that point, I couldn't and still don't understand why people tease and do mean things to each other for "fun." There is no "fun" in destroying someone. There is only the smug power of control. In that fading light I felt my own light dim a bit. I was trying to find a way to feel loved when the afternoon had shown me that they didn't love me. This was the first time that I felt unloved and could not understand it, and my little light was dimmed.

SECTION 2

Starting Point.
This is Real Life!

CHAPTER 3

Learning Zone

Do something uncomfortable today, by stepping out of box, you don't have to settle for what you are—you get to create who you want to become—Howard Walstein

"But let every man prove his own work, and then shall he have rejoicing in himself alone and not in another." (Galatians 6:4)

Learning Zone: a place where we are tested—a place to prove ourselves: if we will be willing to choose right from wrong; a place to choose our response and reactions to life. Here we are vulnerable. Our weaknesses are revealed, yet through our weaknesses, our strengths are revealed, and we gain wins and learning. In our vulnerability, we learn the true meaning of courage of bravery, and we learn how to overcome the challenges that we face. We can always be guided by light, by God, in the Learning Zone. He never leaves us, although we may struggle to learn the reason for being there in the first place. The Learning Zone is where a lot of life happens—but not all of life.

In Galatians 6:4 it says: "But let every man prove his own work, and then shall he have rejoicing in himself alone and not in another." This life is a testing ground a place to prove our worth our light, a place where we have the agency to make choices of how we respond or react to life. Life is not meant to be free from pain, from heartache, from grief, or from sickness, but we have a choice to how we respond to this. We can prove ourselves in authentic ways, meaning that we will learn from the opposition in all things, or hide in fear and not learn, be proven, or grow.

Since the Learning Zone is a proving ground, there are six things that happen to us here (these are not placed in any order). 1) **Hecklers,** 2) **Shame Shadow©,** 3) **Vulnerability Prism,** 4) **Grounding,** and 5) - **Comfort Cage.** The sixth this our underlying power which is our **agency.** The choice is yours on what you will gain in the Learning Zone.

That was a fast and mean definition. Let's take a deeper dive to find out what this looks like.

Remember, we are sent to this earth to prove ourselves to see if we will choose right from wrong, good over evil, and light from the darkness. To see if we will keep getting back up when the challenges of life kick, knock, and punch us down. Or will we race to hide from the challenge? Will we race back to the comfort cage that is inside the Learning Zone each time we feel scared, uncomfortable, or when we want to create an excuse?

Learning Zones allow us to have the most growth of our lives. But growing is terrifying because that means exposing ourselves to new activities, new people, and new experiences. Here is some insight to a Learning Zone I experienced.

Practical Lessons

Point, lift, turn, and stretch, backbend, kick-over, repeat, again and again down the blue and tan mats. I would perform the basics of tumbling repeatedly. My eyes looked up as I stepped off the mat for the hundredth time and I would see her. Her face had soft cheeks, tired eyes, and relaxed brow. She was looking at me then back down at her strong small hands pulling the thread up and down completing the pattern of her embroidery.

She felt my gaze on her and glanced up, nodding to me as if to say, "Keep going, keep practicing, don't give up." Her simple glance empowered me to try again and again; to not give up, working hard until I had mastered the basics, the foundation so that I could really fly one day. She never interfered with the coaching. She trusted them, and she supported me.

My mom would sit for hours with me at the gym, or with my sisters at the pool. Since she was a mother of five children and worked full time, she would sometimes bring projects like the family's ironing pile from home to our practices so that her time would be maximized and not wasted. It was very practical.

It never bothered me that she would do this except for one time. I was at tumbling, and she was where the parents sat, but she was not sitting. She had her ironing board, iron, clothing, and can of starch. Her arm was going back and forth, and back and forth, over stubborn wrinkles as steam would sometimes fly up off the iron in a puff.

I remember the comments of my teammates as my mom pushed the iron back and forth over my dad's church shirts. Their hand motions mimicked and mocked her. Then they snickered and laughed at her. They whispered how embarrassed they would be if their parents brought their ironing to the gym. I could not understand why they were laughing at my mom! I heard the dark voice inside my head agree with them.

Suddenly, a fire lit in my belly because of their laughter! I blurted out, "My mom is helping our family! You shut up!" I must have shrieked a little loudly because it felt like all heads in the gym turned to look at my angry red face. My chest was rising and falling rapidly with heavy-angered breath! As I looked at the three girls who were mocking my mom, I wanted to punch them in the face, but instead turned and ran into the bathroom and locked the door. I had never stood up and shouted out at anyone before.

I understood the family rule: "Nothing happens if nobody's working on it." If there was work to be done, then you did it, and that was what my mom was doing. Why couldn't they understand that? Hot tears were on my cheeks as I stared at the mirror and heard their mocking tone replay in my head. What was so wrong with what she was doing? She had five children, she worked full time, she was a wife to my dad, and she spent time with me! I wiped the tears off my face and opened the door and went back to the tumbling line. I kept my eyes focused on the mat. I didn't look at anyone the rest of the night except for my mom and my coach.

This Learning Zone experience taught me that could take a stand. It taught me I could show a little courage. I could defend and protect others, and I could even "fight" a little. I'd love to report that the teasing and mocking stopped; it didn't. But I knew the right and the wrong of their actions and I chose to take a stand.

In this story we see a few elements of the Learning Zone: 1) Hecklers, 2) Vulnerability Prism, and 3) Grounding. The Hecklers are the ones that point and mock at us. They "know it all." They don't need to be in the fight because it is easier to sit on the sidelines and point out the flaws of everyone else. Those girls in my tumbling class definitely win this label.

I held that vulnerability prism when I decided to make a stand and tell them to "shut up." Maybe I saw a spark of courage and faith. More in-depth about this in chapter 7. And Finally, the grounding was when I had to run into the bathroom and locked the door. I was working through the emotions of calming down because with the anger I felt, I really could have punched them out. But instead I wiped the tears off my face and opened the door and went back to the tumbling line. I kept my eyes focused on the mat. I didn't look at anyone the rest of the night except for my mom and my coach.

I had another option with this story. I could have chosen to run and hide in my comfort cage and just let the teasing go on and on. In my life, I have definitely hidden inside the comfort cage and not wanted to face my challenges. But for some reason I didn't that day. I stood up and took it on.

Goal setting in the Learning Zone

Beep, Beep, BEEP, BEEP, BEEP!! My eyes shot opened and my hand clicked the button on my alarm to OFF. It was 5:17am, time to get up; time for the papers. As I lifted my 16 year-old-self out of my warm cocoon that crisp fall morning, I glanced at my gold medal hanging on my wall just opposite my bed, and I was reminded of why I was getting up. That medal just hung from its red, white, and blue ribbon by a simple pushpin into the cork board. It was my first medal from Nationals. My first National championship in Power Tumbling that I won 3 years before. I had added 2 more medals since then and I was determined that it was not going to be my last.

I pulled on my hat, jacket, and heavy shoes, headed through the hallway, around the corner, and through the bathroom hallway to the garage door. Upon opening the door a wall of frosty air hit me and my breath appeared as steam puffs coming out of my nose. I reached down and grabbed the bundle of newspapers and bags that had been dropped for me to fold and deliver that morning. It was the first part of November and I knew that my drive on the scooter delivering newspapers that morning would be a cold one.

I carried the heavy papers inside and walked back into the kitchen to begin the folding process. Slide, fold, press and rubber band doubled around the paper and stuff into the saddlebag repeated my hands 36 times. Done; now lift and carry back outside. Once the papers were folded and the saddlebag was straddled around the Honda Elite 250, I sat on the scooter and fired it up. The soft putt-putt hum of the gas powered engine was all I could hear in the quiet dark of the morning as I drove off to deliver the morning papers. This scene had been repeated for four years and would continue for another two years.

The money from that paper route helped me pay for my national tumbling competitions. After school, I would go to tumbling practice three days a week for two hours a night for an entire year just to prepare for it.

I would pound, twist, squeeze, lift, and rebound my body as I did tricks down the ten-foot-wide, 120-foot long blue floor over and over again, perfecting my compulsory skill pass, my five-skill pass, and my ten-skill passes. I would practice landings over and over and over again until I could "stick" it. While waiting for my turn down the mat, I would do 40 crunches or 20 shoulder shrugs against the wall to simulate pushing off the tumbling mat and into the air. More! I would think, more! I was driven.

Then waiting in line, I would repeat the skills in my head again and again. It was my self-talk to reinforce the positive work I was doing. The gym was a safe place for me. I would tune out the chitchat of my teammates because I was there to focus on the words of my coach and to improve my skills. I would watch the elite tumblers and set goals that I would be one day be as great as they were. I stayed focused and worked and worked for years. The goal setting and the work paid off because I held four National titles and I had won a silver medal in the 1988 World Games.

Working, goal setting, making a list, accomplishment…it took dedication and drive to have that every day. When I saw the fruits of my labor, I would set my sights even higher and strive to accomplish more ambitious goals. I learned that it takes dedication, determination, and drive to accomplish what you want.

However, I've also learned that there are other factors in life that are out of your control in the Learning Zone, and they often obscure your path as you are trying to accomplish your goals. There was also that dark sharp voice—the Shame Shadow© that, if I paid attention to it, would also make me feel hollow and worthless. In the Learning Zone, I would need to remember my strengths and my weaknesses, knowing that I would be working through both in order to find any success.

Living in the Learning Zone stretches us in ways that we never thought possible, but our Creator KNEW were possible. Learning Zones allow us to have the most growth of our lives. But growing is terrifying because that means exposing ourselves to new activities, new people, and new experiences.

What are some of your Learning Zones you have faced in your lifetime? They will feel like experiences that you learned from. List a few of the LZ's of your life and any of the lessons that you learned there.

Learning Zone

Name the Learning Zones of your Life	Lessons learned from the Learning Zone

CHAPTER 4

Shame Shadow©

You cannot stand in the light while sheltering in the darkness—Anonymous

"And the great dragon was cast out, that old serpent, called the Devil, and Satan, which deceiveth the whole world: he was cast out into the earth, and his angels were cast out with him." (Revelations 12:9)

The Shame Shadow© follows you around everywhere. It will never leave you. But you don't have to look at it or turn to it. You can turn away from it and feel the light of the sun in your face. When we face the light, we are not facing the darkness of the shadow. We are enveloped in the light. The shadow is gone from our view but is still behind us. If we are always looking behind us, we are lost in the darkness of the shadow and we have given it power. However, when we turn from the shadow and face the light in front of us, we are enveloped with Christ's strength and power! We must make a choice: shadow or light? It is a simple one, but we must choose the light!

Shame Shadow©: It is the negative dark voice in our head. You know the one. It's been with since you were a child. It was awakened by an act, by words that someone said, or by an event. It is the voice of the destroyer. The voice of doubt, blame, guilt, and finally, shame.

Shame Shadow© has two ways to talk to you: 1) It says, "You are _____enough" meaning he knows our weaknesses and so he will fill in that blank with something that will really get to us. Or 2) "Who do you think you are?" This also has a wide variety of what it sounds like to us.

To be absolutely clear about the Shame Shadow©. You will *never* get rid of it. Why? Remember in Chapter 1 "opposition in all things?" It will always be there. I named it a shadow for a reason. Shame Shadows© follow you around everywhere. You always have one and it never leaves you. Wow. You might be thinking, "Wait I was looking for hope and light, now you are telling me he will never leave? Great. If that is the truth, then why bother reading more?"

Maybe you thought I was going to tell you "but I am here to show you how you can destroy it!" No. Opposition in this world is sound and true; therefore, it will always be there. But don't give up hope. I will show you and tell you how you can defeat it.

Are you ready for the BIG SHOCKING secret? The number one way to defeat the Shame Shadow©? It comes down to this. We MUST make a choice! That's it. That's the answer. You must choose light or darkness. You must choose good or evil. How? Here it is: as the feeling of the Shame Shadow© trickles over you, you have a choice. Succumb to it or fight it. You can choose to look at it or not. You can choose to turn to darkness or not. You don't have to listen to it! Even though it is always behind you, you have a choice to look at it or turn towards light.

You have the choice to turn away from it and feel the light of the Son in your face. When we face the light, we are not facing the darkness of the shadow. We are enveloped in the light. The shadow is gone from our view. The shadow is behind you. If we are always looking behind us, then we have not understood the light that is in front of us. We must make a choice. It is a simple one, but we must choose the Light!

The choice is simple, but not necessarily easy. So, let's get into this more deeply and find out why the Shame Shadow© says; what it does to us. I'll start with the simple structure that the Shame Shadow© uses for all of us: "You are _____ enough." For you, it might mean you are NEVER, NOT SMART, NOT PRETTY, NOT GOOD, enough etc.

For me this saying of "You are ___ enough" sounded like this to me: *You are TOOO much for others.* For example, *You are too excited. You have too much energy. You have 9 children—too many. Your kids are deaf and have autism. You are too happy. You are too churchy. You are too excited, etc.* This idea of you are TOO much is on the surface when people say it. But what my Shame Shadow© says to me is, "You are too much," which means, "You are unlovable."

The "too much" in my life that makes me feel unlovable comes from a desire to want to please, perfect, and perform— My three deadly "P's. They were the poison— that stuff you drink slowly, that goes deep, deep into the bones and takes years to kill you. Why are the three "P's" deadly? Because the Shame Shadow© started to whisper these to me at a young age. Remember the story about the stuffed animals? I couldn't **please** my sisters, and felt unlovable.

If I didn't perform, then who could see the work I did? My tumbling, my paper route, my schoolwork. The Shame Shadow© had been trying to convince me from a young age that all of these were crucial to do in order to understand where my value was. I must perform in order to be loved. The shadow convinced me that my performance equaled how much I was loved. If I wanted more love, then I must do and perform all that I can in order to have love.

If I didn't perfect, then I couldn't be loved. If I didn't please others and let them have what they wanted, then I was NOT being nice or a good girl. If I didn't do everything to a **perfection** level, then what value did I hold? Afterall, people want the best—at least that is what the Shame Shadow© would say again and again to me. Through the experiences I had, I then started to tie them to my value/worth/light. I thought that I needed the three P's in order to be lovable. Afterall, that is what the Shame Shadow© had been whispering to me.

Pleasing: This took my desire to want to do good and be good into, "You are not worthy enough and you will never be enough," because the goal posts or the home base for the win was constantly being moved by the people I was trying to please. I could never satisfy the requirements for everything they wanted because there is always one more thing to do. I could never reach the "pleasing" goal line. I tied my worth/ light to this.

Hide and Seek

Soft cool grass cushioned my small feet with each running step I took. The coolness of each blade of grass was so different compared to the heat radiating from the concrete of "home base." Pinks and deep yellows painted a pallet in the western sky and the first two or three stars dared to shine as twilight settled in around us. Laughter and squeals of excitement skipped off the warmth of the summer air, quickly followed by a short "Shh-quiet down."

"....seven, eight, nine, ten! Ready or not, here I come!" Suddenly my feet left the heated concrete and plunged back onto the cool grass, but this time my seven-year-old legs were pumping faster and faster and like a blur they blended into the darkening surroundings. I found my hiding spot and melted into the darkness waiting for the seeker to find me. I was perfectly camouflaged and so, I waited.

Suddenly a flash of blue and white caught my eye. I saw my younger brother's feet run past me! My heart jumped, making a thundering noise against my chest and pounding in my head! *Calm*, I told myself. *Take a breath! Stay calm.* He must have left the comfort of his hiding place to find another, or to "kick the can" to free my sister who might have been caught. I closed my eyes and took in a breath and silently released it into the heat of the summer night. My thundering heart began to beat more slowly as I settled back into my hiding place.

I sat staring out from my dark hiding hole across the lawn. I saw her—my oldest sister—the seeker. She suddenly stepped toward the black hole in which I was hiding. Her silhouette was perfectly outlined in blackness as she continued to move towards me. I caught my breath in my throat making sure silence was the only sound I produced. She ran at first and then stepped closer and closer! With each step my throat was closing in tighter and tighter so that I didn't make a sound.

Suddenly, with her hand reaching into the dark hole she turned away and ran towards home base! Tink, clang, ting, clang, clang, clang, rang out the sound of the can as it skipped across the pavement. My little brother must have reached the base and freed my two other sisters in jail. Yes! I was never going to be caught! I was going to win the game!

Winning for me when playing "kick the can," with my older sisters was something that never happened. I was always searching for my place in the group to belong too. I was searching for that love of others; I wanted that feeling of love of pleasing someone or that what I did mattered and would please them so I'd be accepted by my family.

I wanted a sense of belonging. When one does not belong in a family, life can get really lonely because family is the foundation for belonging. When we feel a sense of loss of connection with it, our most primal self seeks out again and again to connect for our very survival. I could see my sisters' connection and relationship with each other, and I wanted that connection so badly that my desire to please them pushed me nearly every day to find a way.

But I learned that I had two choices: I could continue to try to please them and get their approval, or I could just stay out of their way. My sisters were still my sisters; they were just not going to be my companions during my childhood. They were not interested in having me be with them as that third wheel. I tearfully and painfully began to accept it. The Shame Shadow© would whisper how I failed...I couldn't even please my own family.

Performance: I love action and take action in all that I do every day. However, in my performance I was trying to prove that I was lovable by my actions. I had many places in my life that I performed in school, church, and tumbling. I was a power tumbler (think gymnastics the floor exercise but without music and dance—just straight tumbling), so in my competitions, my performance counted!

The Grand Finale!

It was July 1991, and the heat in Louisiana was making my warm-up pants stick to my thighs. My teammates and I sat on the big blue tumbling floor stretching and preparing for our turn to warm up our skills on the floor. This was it; this was my National championship where I was searching for my 5th title. The signal by the judge was given that it was our turn to warm up.

Run, skip, twist, double twist, turn, whip-back, whip-back, double twist, spot the landing, look, stick. I repeated this for my five-trick skill three times. Run, skip Double twist, twist, whip-back, twist, whip-back, whip-back, twist, twist, double full, punch front, spot the landing, stick! Yes! Finally, I completed one of my second-skills passes. I was having trouble with my second and third trick connecting. I wasn't bounding correctly—my timing was off. I only had two more warm-up passes left, and if I wasn't hitting, I could always go to my alternate pass.

With my next warm-up I used my alternate pass—I hit it! Now I had a decision to make: to try my hardest pass one more time or stick with my alternate pass and compete a cleanly executed one. The dark voice appeared. "You should prove it." Suddenly it was like dark silence had rushed the scene that was all around me.

I was suddenly this small figure in a vast darkening room with a large shadow in the corner hissing, "prove it." From that empty dark hollow place, I was suddenly back with the colors, lights, and competitors. I was fighting with myself and struggling to know which pass to compete. Time was running. With each step I was walking closer and closer to my coach. With each step that voice was saying "prove it, prove it, prove it."

I approached the mat—only one warm up left—do the clean pass and compete tomorrow. Do the hard pass and Win! Step, step, run, run, as I entered into the air, I chose to practice for the last warm-up my harder pass. Run, skip, half-twist, double twist, full, slip—- crash...ug! And gasps from the crowd. That was the last pass! Warm-ups were over.

My coach met me as I stood off the mat. The words of coaching, of trusting in those words of hers, were quick, "Do the clean pass! You are *not* ready."

"But!" I protested, "But, I want to show that I can hit this pass in competition! It is what I have been working for!" I was surprised at my own forcefulness, and so was my coach. She looked at me deeply, and for a long time.

I heard myself promising that I could do it, that I could hit it, that I could be the one to hit this pass in competition. I wanted to prove that my hard work had not been for nothing—that I could hit my pass because it had the hardest difficulty. My coach looked at me and held my eyes for a long while. "Do the clean pass." I stopped talking. She smiled. "You need more practice. Do the clean pass." I half nodded, turned and walked off the mat.

I followed the other competitors to the waiting area for my turn. The voice kept saying to myself that I could do the harder pass—after all—I hit it eight out of ten times. Those odds were pretty good. I knew I could hit it! "Do the clean pass," kept repeating in my mind. It was like a small voice in the room of hundreds of other shouting voices. It was quickly quieted and soon fell silent. The shadow's voice was sharp in my head, *Prove it!* I decided to go for it to really impress the judges; after all, I was going for my 5th straight championship title and I wanted it to be my statement. I fell into the Shame Shadow's control again. I felt I could prove it!

Soon my name was called out. This was the first of three passes for that day's competition. It was my turn for my compulsory pass. I ran, skipped, and completed the pass with flawless execution. I was clean, tight, and stuck the landing. "There! See! You can do it!" The small voice was ringing clearly. "You even stuck the landing." I was smiling and I looked at my coach. She smiled back.

I quickly turned to ready myself for my second pass—my five-trick pass. I waited my turn until the judge gave me the salute. I smiled and raised arm in a return salute. I felt my legs begin to pump into a run, then I skipped, half-twist, double twist, whip-back, full twist, double twist. Land! I hit it! I hit the harder pass! I did it! It was a little under rotated however, but it was a clean pass. I did it! I did it! I quickly looked up and met my coach's eyes. She smiled! It was a great moment! I'd hit two of my three passes. I can do it with my clean pass!

Then the shadow crept in right before my third and final pass. "Prove it." I felt a creepy inky blackness start to flow from the corner of my mind. "Prove it." I looked for my coach. She was coaching my teammate. "Prove it." I shut my eyes, took a deep breath, and my eyes shot open again looking for my coach. I felt the doubt creep into my heart. Time froze for a few seconds and I felt that I was going to fail. "Prove it." I searched for my coach one more time. Then like a flash of light *Do the clean pass*, hit me. But just as any flash of light ends, darkness replaces it. "If you don't try, you will fail!"

My flash of light and prayerful heart was silenced, and the dark voice took over: "Hit the pass." *If I didn't, I would become the failure. Breathe...wait for the signal from the judge ...breathe, there's the signal...raise my salute*, and I ran down the floor. Run, skip, half-twist, double twist, full...pound... no mat under my feet! Then suddenly slap on my neck, roll to shoulder, hip, thigh, and momentum stopped. I was on my side, off the blue mat and on the platform.

I pulled myself off the ground. I raised up my arms and my hands flicked in a final salute to the judges and stepped off the platform. It was over. I was in stunned silence. I had to walk the long walk back to the waiting area. Step, step, step, all the eyes from the audience were still looking at me. Step, step, step. Silence was still with me. Step, step, step. It was over. Step, step, step. I had fallen. Step, step, step. I had failed. Step, step, step. Suddenly a piercing voice, came into my heart, "Failure! What kind of performance was that? You can never compete again, after all, who will root for a loser?" Step, step, step. And with that, I decided never to return to a competition again—and I never competed again.

What had happened? How did I miss my feet? How did I crash? This was not me! I never crashed in competition. I learned the precise formula for setting goals and achieving them. Perseverance and drive are a powerful strategy and one that proved for me to be very successful. But what happened in Louisiana taught me that I had listened to the wrong voice, instead of listening to my heart and my coach. I had been arrogant and full of myself—I wanted to show off and, in that moment, and I failed.

Perfecting: My Shame Shadow's© personal favorite. The Shame Shadow pushed this poison on me, and it was trying to push it toward my destruction. What perfectionism demanded was that you must accomplish even the unattainable goals. "Be ye therefore perfect, even as your Father in Heaven is perfect." (Matthew 5:48).

The Shame Shadow used this verse again and again nearly to my destruction. Because it was always accompanied by failure. I did not understand that perfection was not obtainable here on earth, but that it would come eventually. You must keep going: repent when you fall, forgive others when they fall, and endure to the end. But, no. The Shame Shadow would not let this drop. It demanded perfection in the way I looked, how much I weighed, and how I was to act—like I was always happy and in control of my life was the power behind this goal.

However, we are *not perfect* and never can be in this life. Each time I stepped in the Learning Zone to "win the title of perfection" I would come out feeling lost, fearful, and like a failure because I disappointed so many. The shadow would say, "unlovable" and that would twist in my head because I could NEVER obtain perfection. The Shame Shadow just laughed.

From not being able to please, perform, or perfect anything the way that the Shame Shadow© kept demanding it from me, I turned to control. I needed to find something in the darkness of this shadow.

Food Fight

Food was something that I had in abundance growing up, and that I used to nourish my body, but at one point it became my source of control. When I was in high school, I was fascinated with the idea of control. There were parts of my life that were out of control, so I decided to deal with it by turning to food as something to control. I guess you could say I became anorexic by choice. I knew about how to ration food, look like you were eating in front of many, but to make sure that you were always busy and skipping meals when no one was looking. It was so easy.

The hunger pains were the reward for controlling the food and after a while they would actually give me a sense of accomplishment. It is a sick way to live, but when one wants control, for me, it was the fix that was the easiest.

Slice, slice, slice came the sound of the sharp knife against the plump red skin of the tomato. "Thinner!" harshly whispered Shame. I stopped my knife mid-slide and looked at the thin slices that were nearly transparent.

I picked up the knife again, ready to try to please my Shame Shadow, but then I thought, *I only sliced four slices just enough to spread out on a plate.* My shaking hand picked up the window thin slice and laid it out on the plate. I place the fourth slice down on the plate. *There* I think. *That is one more than yesterday. I deserve to eat one more. I can enjoy it.* Right after that thought, another voice sliced across me, "So much food. I thought you had more control."

I had three slices of tomato on a plate and I began to tremble as I held the fourth slice debating whether I should lay it out on the plate! Then the Shame struck again. "Are you really going to eat that much?" I stood there frozen at what Shame said to me. It was scoffing at me. I felt that prick go right to my heart and I felt a little more of my light dim. I put one back and thought, *There; I'll just eat three.* I looked up for approval, but all was silent.

To recap, the Shame Shadow© follows you around everywhere. Just like in reality your shadow is always there when light shines. It is "opposition in all things." It will never leave you. But the trick with the shadow is that you don't have to look at it or turn to it. You can turn away from it and feel the light of the sun in your face.

When we face the light, we are not facing the darkness of the shadow. We are enveloped in the light. The shadow is gone from our sight because we are facing the light. The shadow stays behind you. If we are always looking behind us, we are lost in the darkness of the shadow and we have given it power. However, when we turn from the shadow and face the light in front of us, we are enveloped with His strength and power! We must make a choice: shadow or light? It is a simple one, but we must choose the light!

Shame Shadow© what does it say to you? Write or draw it out.

What are your three "p's" of poison? Please, Perform, Perfect? Write or draw it out.

CHAPTER 5

Fallen Angel

Sometimes as children, we are exposed to and experience hard and challenging events. They can take a lifetime to heal from. But there is always hope. Carl Jung said:

"I am not what happened to me, I am what I choose to become." —Carl Jung

"But whoso shall offend one of these little ones which believe in me, it were better for him that a millstone were hanged about his neck, and that he were drowned in the depth of the sea." (Matthew 18:6).

This chapter is a foundational piece of my life's story, but not a defining piece of my story. All tragedy can be learned from and it doesn't have to define us. This story shaped me, but I have taken the events that happened in the past, learned from them, and slowly I understood how I could choose who I wanted to become.

Fallen Angel

As a young girl, jumping on the trampoline and flipping into the air gave me a sense of freedom, a sense of flying, and a sense of power. I could manipulate my body into spirals, flips, and twists, and it was something that I was good at. This was something I could do better than anyone else in my family. I would spend hours on the black stretchy mat flying through the air. It gave me a rush and a thrill to do something that my sisters couldn't do. However, the only problem was, I didn't have a trampoline in my yard. But the family next door did.

Bounce, bounce, bounce, bounce! I powered my energy from my strong legs into the black stretchy mat. Then looking at the sky I would spin upward with streaks of blue then white, and then down to see the black mat again. Over and over my legs pumped the pushed and pointed the energy into my flips. Day after day I would return to the trampoline and work on my tricks. Again, and again, I would jump, flip, twist, and practice perfect landings.

I returned to my neighbor's yard, again and again, day after day for weeks. The black stretchy mat would bend with my weight and then returned the energy through my tight legs, pumping me into the air, where my body would somersault, and spin. I would spot the mat and land arms raised, my audience in my mind's eye clapping. My mind was powerful, and my neighbor's yard had become my second gym.

Then one summer day, I had arrived early in the morning to practice, flip and soar on the trampoline. I started practicing my routine as usual. Jump, jump, jump, bound, flip, twist, bound, flip, tuck, bound, flip pike, bound, flip layout, bound flip, twist. Again, and again, I practiced. Nothing was out of the ordinary until I decided to dismount off the trampoline onto the grass. Bound, flip half-twist, fly and I landed on soft grass, tumbling head over heels and stretched and laid on the soft cool grass. I giggled, and took a deep breath, and sighed.

The sky was above me, the grass was beneath me, and I rolled over to push myself up, when something white caught my eye near the corner of the wooded yard. Curious, I walked over and saw a beautiful patch of trees, with light filtering through the dense green leaves. Why had I never seen this little nook of my neighbor's yard before? Had my eyes only focused on the trampoline? Possibly. After all, my seven-year-old mind was solely focused on practicing my flips, spins, and twists.

My feet carried me step by step into the sunbeams that filtered through the trees in this small patch of wood. My eyes scanned the tops of the trees, the midline of the growth, and then to the undergrowth of soft dirt and the small nook. As I continued to scan the undergrowth, I saw a small porcelain angel figurine with a gentle smile, wings bent in and arms stretched out. The one soft sunbeam lit the tips of the wings and the outstretched hand. In that hand, light bounced off a glittery foil wrapped candy. *A gift from the angel*, I thought to myself. It was magical.

My creative imagination went wild! I could see myself as a fairy queen ready to rule this little kingdom. How had I never seen this before? This had to be my little secret. My heart skipped and it sent a little giggle up into my throat. I quickly ran home with my little foil wrapped treat in my hand. All I could think of was that I had found my secret place—my Angel Nook.

I set a rule for myself that I would only be allowed into the nook if I jumped and flipped and twisted on the trampoline. I must work first and then have my reward. The excitement that filled my little soul made me squeal and giggle even more. I had a place. I had something special. I had something just for me ...or so I thought.

I returned to the trampoline again and again and practiced and flipped, then tipped-toed and slipped into the nook.

Sometimes there was a foil-wrapped treat and sometimes not. However, on this particular day in the nook, movement caught my eye. As I turned, I was startled to see someone standing there. He gave me a wink and a quick bow. I was still surprised to see someone there, but I returned a fast flash of a smile and curtsied back. His smile split across his face. He said he had loved watching me flip, soar, and fly through the air, and that he had been watching for weeks.

I could feel my neck rising with color until it splashed over onto my freckled face. I had an admirer. He said that I could continue to jump on the trampoline and come into the garden anytime I wanted—and that he wouldn't spoil my secret. My heart was still beating fast and I didn't know what to say. He seemed to see my hesitation and he reached into his pocket and pulled out a foil wrapped candy. I took a quick gasp of breath. The candy. He had been placing it on the outstretched hand of the angel. He had been the one creating the magic of Angel Nook for me.

Out of surprise, I was suddenly pulled toward his hand and I took the candy. I looked at him again; I thanked him, and he smiled. I didn't want to break the magic of the moment, so I turned on the spot, and skipped my way out of the garden back toward my home. Just before rounding the corner of the yard I glanced back and gave a quick wave, which he returned. I knew who my Angel was in my Angel Nook, and I vowed to return and play one of my games in the private secluded garden.

I returned, again and again, to jump and perform, and this time to hear the praises and awe of my neighbor. It was so much better to perform for someone, so my trips to the neighbor's house became more and more frequent. Always at the end of my tumbling performances, we would make a quick trip into the garden where I would pretend to be the queen and he would be the knight in shining armor.

Our games went on for weeks that summer. The games lead to climbing, racing, and piggy-back riding as he rescued me from the dragons. In the end, we always hugged, and he would praise me for being strong and for always winning. Until one day he asked me for a kiss.

It is always proper for the queen to bestow a kiss to the brave knight who has saved her from the dragons, isn't it? As I bent to give the kiss, my knight held me into an embrace and began to touch me in a way that was different from anything I had experienced before. I didn't fight. I didn't shout. I did nothing but just allowed the touching and kissing to happen. And he whispered to me, "My little mouse—this will be our secret." Then he squeezed me in a crushing hug and forcefully whispered, "It's your fault. You tempted me. Just know that if you tell, I'll tell that it was your fault." He then released me and gave me some candy. He winked and bowed his head to me with his finger to his lips, reinforcing to me that I should stay quiet.

My legs still stood frozen and heavy on the spot. He walked away, and I just stood there, partially naked. What had happened? I pulled my pants back up, turned and drug my feet across the ground and back toward home. I felt confused, ugly, bad, dirty. My fault? My fault? Suddenly I heard a voice, "It was your fault you know. You tempted him." Then I felt a darkness creep in like a shadow dimming my light. I was just playing a game. What was that part of the game? I just wanted to tumble and get some candy. *What had happened?* Was all I could repeat over and over again in my head. Again, the voice said, "Your fault."

Like any child, I was naturally trusting, and he had won my trust. He had won my affection and my reassurance through the weeks of praise and attention that he had bestowed upon me.

Let's check off the three P's: pleasing others—yes, he paid attention to me so I did what I thought would please him. Perform? Yes, I would work on routines to make sure that I could perform at the right time! Perfect? I...I... would have to keep this secret with PERFECTION because it was my fault! I knew that it was my fault. The Shame Shadow© emphasized that.

The acts of that summer happened repeatedly, again and again, not because I wanted it to, but because he needed it to. They lasted until deep into the fall where the leaves could no longer hide the acts that took place there, and it stopped.

These were the thoughts in my head, and they continued for years afterward. Therapy over the years told me that I was a child, and as a child, I didn't know any better. But the guilt from the voice in my head made me feel so stupid and foolish to have let it happen. I simply had trusted him, and he took that trust and twisted it to his advantage.

Once he had had enough, I was rubbish—tossed aside like an empty can who's sweet contents had been eagerly drained to quench the desired thirst. Once the last drop had been consumed the empty vessel was then twisted and crushed in those teenager's hands and flung out to scrape along the pavement to be kicked down the road by a few others later in my life. I was left so confused, and all I gained was a sense that I would have to keep this secret perfectly, because it was my fault.

I was a crushed can of trash. The hollowness and emptiness inside filled every void of my young life. I had a crushing secret and shame began to eat away my happy little spirit like drops of acid rain, bit by bit. Over time it would erode my light into a grey and dimming day that slipped into darkness. My trust had been twisted and warped and I had a crushing secret to keep. The Shame Shadow© dimmed a large portion of my light. I had become a fallen Angel.

For twelve years following that summer I held that secret. It was the perfect little way for the Shame Shadow© to wreak havoc with my light, my worth, and my soul. This Chapter shared a deep wounding event, but there is hope. The Fallen

Angel was not for a lifetime; it was only for as long as I gave it power. If you have had times in your life that feel like you were a fallen Angel, I encourage you to write about them. Healing happens as we are able to write the words and hear ourselves work through the pain. Feel free to write what you wish here.

CHAPTER 6

Comfort Cage.
The Lie.

Denial is the worst kind of lie because it is the lie you tell yourself. —Michelle Homme

"A false witness shall not be unpunished, and *he that* speaketh lies shall not escape" (Proverbs 19:5).

Comfort. What do you think of when you hear that word? A place that is plush, full of warmth, soft textures, soft light, maybe something soothing to eat—sweet or savory? Comfort. We all seek it, want it, try to hold onto it, and in desperation, we fight to have it in our lives. We will even numb ourselves to try to find a sense of false comfort. Even when we are numb, we are fighting hard to make sure that we put at bay the feelings that put us in vulnerable places.

Where is the Comfort Cage found? Where does it reside? It is actually found inside the Learning Zone. We run toward the false sense of comfort we think we will find there. It looks like it has pillows, cushions, soft lighting, and a place to stay and be safe. However, once we are inside, we notice that soft light is filtered and suddenly we notice that there are bars all around us trapping us inside!

Just as we turn around to run out the bars slide shut— clicking and locking into place. Trapped! Some think let's just stay here. We are fine inside here. At least we are safe from what is happening out there. We can hang out here. We might even think that staying in the Learning Zone exposes us to experiencing the Shame Shadow. So, if we stay in our comfort cage, he can't get us in here.

As you are symbolically fluffing your pillows and trying to make this cage as comfortable as possible, you notice that you really aren't getting comfortable. It feels like there is always some kind of annoying chill in the air. The longer you stay here, you begin to notice that the bars have words printed on them. They are made from fear, and out of our pain. As you read more words you notice the lies that are etched into the metal. As you read them your brain seems to echo them—like you've heard and have told yourself for years.

You feel your knees buckle and give way until you find yourself on the floor. You suddenly notice a dark shadow and the echo of the lies, the doubt, all that you lack comes through the spaces of the bars toward you. The deepest feelings of your fear, your pain, and your doubt is suddenly amplified. You can feel yourself start to rationalize and tell yourself more lies, and now you're seriously trapped within your cage of comfort.

Even with all of that happening, some won't leave their cage. As backward as it seems, they fear the unknown in the Learning Zone even more than the pain or doubt. Many choose to stay in the cage. The anxiety and fear grip them! They can't go out of the Comfort Cage to face the unknown. They are convinced that they will face possible destruction, and so they grip the bars of the cage tighter and tighter trying to ensure their pain, fear, and anxiety keep them trapped there.

If you leave the comfort cage because you want to form relationships with others, this may cause a deep fear of getting hurt. It is taking a risk to even love someone. I mean it is easier to just stay with what you know because loving others is taking a BIG risk. They might not return that love. They might not be willing to risk things themselves. All of that is justified. Yet as humans, we are social creatures and we must connect and respond with others to feel complete.

You've heard all your life about the comfort zone. It feels like a place that we want to get back to if we are outside of it. A comfort zone feels like a place that will provide comfort. But really it is a lie, and like more lies, the entanglement and strangulation squeeze out all truth! The comfort zone really is a Comfort Cage! How? Because you are trapped. You are not progressing. You are not growing. You are just stuck.

At first, it feels like comfort, but soon you realize that comfort is false. Over time you realize that you are actually trapped there. You see the bars made out of your fears, your worries, and your lies as you slowly turn around from reading everything on the bars and find you are face to face with your Shame Shadow©. It is willing to embrace you and tries to offer comfort but as it touches you, all you feel is cold and darkness.

Suddenly you want to bolt out of there! You want to run, but, if you open the cage, you will find hard work and a learning zone in front of you. That is just as equally terrifying. So, you opt to stay in your comfort cage thinking, *At least I can't get hurt in here.* But that too, is a lie, and you begin to justify your comfort.

Justifying Comfort

It's ok, I keep repeating to myself. *It's gonna be ok.* I look at my purse, counting the government issued food stamps. I'll make it last. I mean, I know my husband is doing another construction job, and then he might get paid. I'll just figure it out and make things work. Again, I use rationalization about my financial circumstances to try to comfort me.

You see, I knew how to ration food, measure food down to the last spoonful, and how to control my hunger pains. I knew how to do all of this based on my years of anorexia. I knew how to control my food intake, but now, when it changes and becomes a fight for every scrap of food for the family, it became terrifying. My family, my children needed to eat. When I was anorexic, it was for total control, but now the lack of food was because I had no control! Each time I would have to go grocery shopping, I lied to myself, seeking comfort that I would have enough food for the family.

We always had something to eat, but it was rationed down to the last bite. It had to be. I would take what little money plus WIC (Women Infant Children food support) coupons and try to make the food stretch over a month at a time. I spent the money on food, for the basics. It was so small and meager; I was completely embarrassed. I would make everything I could from scratch. I would put aside $6 dollars a month for staples like flour, sugar, yeast, salt, canned soups, or Top Ramen. It would take about 3 months to save enough to get the staples and I would have to stretch it to last the next 3 months.

Once a month I could go to the store and buy these staples to last for the month, and then our weekly shopping trip was with WIC coupons. I would tell myself we were alright. I was deep in the comfort cage. With each justification and rationalization, the bars of the comfort cage would strengthen.

Symbolically, I would hold onto the bars, trying to find comfort as each new lie was told.

My children's birthdays would fall on or close to major holidays. I would be so grateful to organize a party and I would manipulate the conversation so that we would end up having the party at my in-laws, or my family members. I would organize it to be a potluck to ensure that my children would have a special day and would feel that they didn't go without on their birthday. I would bring something I could make from scratch, like a loaf of bread but they would bring food like meat, chips, cake and ice cream! It would be a day full of good things to eat, and I would live in that three-hour moment because I knew the next day it would be back to rationing and justifying my comfort.

But I kept up the lies to give me comfort. That comfort kept me away from the reality that my former spouse was not going to be able to provide. I hoped that a miracle would happen. I did all I could with government subsidies and just wished the construction jobs would come for us. I wished that the money he made in construction would be given to me to run the house, and when it wasn't, I justified and lied more to myself and more bars were formed from the Comfort Cage.

How many of you have a Comfort Cage? What are the lies that you tell yourself so that you don't have to go back out into the Learning Zone and become vulnerable? Do you ask yourself why you will justify and rationalize? As a victor over domestic violence, I can tell you my reasons for staying in my Comfort Cage. I feared to step out back into the Learning Zone because I would be so vulnerable that my life and the lives of my children might actually be in peril. I knew the danger within the comfort of the cage. But outside of the cage, I could not predict it.

Most of the time our Comfort Cage is there to help us avoid growth. If we can find contentment in our tiny cage, then why would we leave it? If we can tell ourselves enough lies to decorate the place - again, why would we leave it? We are in denial of where we are in our journey. We can't make any progress. But, if we are willing to leave the cage, and venture into the Learning Zone, there might be a way out of the hell we have convinced ourselves is comfortable.

Out of Jail

I will never forget the date of July 2, 2006. The day was busy with five kids ages one to seven years old, missing socks, dishes in the sink, and diaper rash on my baby, but there was also excitement. I had begged a neighbor to watch my kids because I had an appointment. I climbed up into the old green van and glanced at the gas gauge. One-fourth tank of gas. This would get me down the canyon and into the city. I was headed to the university to meet with the dean in the English department.

After paying for my parking pass and shutting the door to the van, I turned and looked at all the windows on the building. I wondered, *Will I find the answers I am looking for?* Upon the quick four-floor elevator ride, I stepped outside at the ding of the bell. The hallway was empty and yet I remember the air smelling like old books. That made me smile because I felt a little of my college years flutter up reminding me about the hours, I would spend in the library studying. I quietly walked toward the directory.

I looked at the number of the office I had scribbled down on a sheet of paper and matched it with the number 442. I felt my feet move in that direction toward the office. The door was slightly ajar, so I softly knocked and slipped into the office, where I was greeted by the secretary. She asked for my name, scanned down her paper, found my name and confirmed my appointment. She picked up the receiver and said, "Your 2:00 appointment is here." She flashed a quick smile, gave me the look-over and went back to typing.

I heard a firm but nice voice say, "Come in," and I felt my feet follow that command, even though I was second guessing my move to meet with the dean of the English department. Doubt and denial were really plunging in on my head through the Shame Shadow©, and I knew I was going to have a fight on my hand.

"Hi. April, right? Please, have a seat." I did and looked about the tiny room. "I see on my notes you wanted to discuss what it would take to become an English teacher, since you already have your Bachelor of Science in English, is that right?" I stammered, out, "Yes."

"And you are here to find out about the 'Hemmingway Teaching Program?'"

"Yes," I answered. She continued, "Can you share with me your reasons for why you want to become a teacher?" I was not prepared for her to ask me a question like that. I just thought she would say, "Take this class, and this class, then you need to do some student teaching, and then you can get a job." No, that was not what happened.

"I..." I started, "I want to be a teacher so that I can provide for my family." *There*, I thought. *That was straightforward. I told her why.* But she was not satisfied and plunged in deeper with, "What are your family's needs?" This question was like pulling on my emotional supports that were holding back the flood of tears that was ready to rupture.

"I am a mother of five children," I started, and then my voice wavered. Three of my children have autism, so I need to find classes I can take around my family's needs." She looked at me with her blue eyes and her strong cheekbones and just sat there. I could feel the welling of tears start in my left eye and I was begging that it would just stay there and not fall. She stood up and walked around the large heavy oak desk and shut the door. I was beginning to panic and feel like I was in the principal's office.

She returned to her desk and her expression had changed. She put on her reading glasses and started to type up something on the computer. I sat in silence not knowing what was going to happen next. Finally, after some length of time, she turned away from her screen, took off her glasses and looked me dead in the eye.

"You would not be a fit for the Hemmingway Program." Her delivery was flat. I felt like her tone of voice was, "Too bad it's not going to happen."

"I figured that this would be a long shot," I blurted out, and I started to get up because I could feel the emotion rising and the tears falling.

"No, please, sit." she said. "You would not be a fit for the Hemmingway Program because it would take 2 years to complete and you would not be able to teach until the program was completed." I quickly blinked. She went on, "You don't have the time to waste on a program like ours. You need a program that will give you an income right away. Something tells me you need it."

My voice was caught in my throat and with that last sentence, "Something tells me you need it," my tear in the right eye fell. "I was looking up your old transcripts. You are a great student and it looks like you have the ability to be a teacher, but not through our program." Again, I was going to stand and thank her, but she waved me down a second time. I was thinking to myself, *What more does she have to say to me*? If the Hemmingway Program isn't right, then what?

She continued, "You need a teaching certification program that you can do *while* you are teaching." My eyebrows narrowed into a question and my brain thought, *Wait...what?* Did she say I could be a teacher while I was in a program—like get paid and still go to school? My confused look must have communicated more, and she said, "You need a certification program and a master's level in Special Education." I felt my mouth fall slightly open.

"You need skills that can help your kids, give you an income, and still take the courses you need to complete the program. You won't find that here. You need to go to a different school." She slid over a piece of paper with the school's name and number on it to call. She continued, "Here is another number to call. It is a scholarship program. Call for information about the scholarship after you learn about the program." I looked up at her, which triggered the other tear to fall and slide down my cheek. I swallowed hard to say thank you. I still couldn't. She smiled back. We just sat in her office for a time while I was taking all of this in.

I took the piece of paper and looked at the second number. Was this really the answer? A program I where I could teach, be in school, have the schedule be just right for my family, and have it paid for? I looked back in her blue eyes and with a shaky voice, I thanked her. She stuck her hand out and shook mine. As I stood up a third time, she said, "Some answers don't come in the way you think, but when they do, follow them."

I have reflected on that miracle that happened in the office hundreds of times over the years. It was so symbolic. I felt that I had just been handed the keys that unlocked my comfort cage. I felt like the rusty bars of doubt, lies, and victimhood slid open, giving me a clear path to walk into the Learning Zone. Was I ready to try the Learning Zone? Was I brave enough to grab hold of the Vulnerability Prism (chapter 8)? With my first step out of the Comfort Cage, I was willing to try. I told myself I was ready for the "learns" ahead, and with the faith of a child, I took the next step out of her office and into the next phase of my life.

What is your Comfort Cage made out of? List your bars that trap you in your comfort Cage.

CHAPTER 7

Hecklers

As a heckler to deny himself or his company. They usually appear to be anonymous.—Judi Moreo

"Judge not, that ye be not judged" (Matthew 7: 1)

Hecklers. You know who they are. They are those people who watch how the shadow can get to you and then they shout out and increase and emphasize your shame. They have all the answers and will tell you over and over again all about your flaws. They will never approach the Learning Zone. Why should they? They can comment from the side, get right to the heart of you, and not have to get dirty in the Learning Zone. Here is the crux of it all, when we choose to listen to them, we have just given them power over us.

Do you know the Hecklers in your life? A better question to ask is, "What do your Hecklers say to you? Are they pushing your buttons? Do they know exactly what to say to get to you? How do they have that power? Afterall, they are not in the

Learning Zone with you. They are on the outside looking in. If you fall into the pleasing, performing and perfecting trap from the Shame Shadow© then the Hecklers know exactly how to push your buttons because you have essentially told them by how you respond and react to others. They have a load of power over you.

In my book Pinpoints of Light, I share all about my first marriage: how I was in an abusive relationship for 9 years and finally was able to get out. But prior to getting out, in my seventh year of marriage, I actually was able to separate from my former spouse for a few months. I was free and clear of him, but I felt the tug to return. I was gutted by the guilt of the Shame Shadow©, therefore, I was an easy target for Hecklers.

Ice Cream Pity

Valentine's Day. A day for love, wedding, for dates, for romance, or for celebrating the loneliest day of the year, as it was for me on February 14, 2005. After 8 years of living in an abusive marriage, I was newly separated from my husband. The mental, physical, and financial abuse had taken a toll on me. After his arrest and charge of DUI and possession of drug paraphernalia, I finally had the courage to separate from him. I moved myself and my children into a basement apartment and tried to pick up the pieces of my shattered life. I had 4 children and was pregnant with my fifth child.

On February 14, 2005, a night for romance, for renewal of vows, for recommitment of relationships, all of which had been shattered in my own life, there was a ray of hope with this night. I was going to take advantage of this. My son's school wanted to give parents a night off on that Valentine's Day. If we had done all of our volunteering, they would offer two hours of free babysitting! My neighbor had been kind enough to give me $10 to put some gas in my van so that I could get down the canyon to enjoy this night and I took full advantage of this. I remember coasting down the canyon as much as possible to save gas. I needed this two-hour break from life so badly. I was maybe a little too thrilled to drop my kids off at Canyon View for the staff, but once I did, I was out of there.

Where would I go? What was my plan? A movie? Dinner? No, instead, I drove to a furniture store just to enjoy being in the beauty of the storeroom. I know, I know. It sounds a little strange but let me share some background about this. My grandparents owned a furniture store called Tribe's Furniture. As a kid, I loved going into the storeroom and looking at all the displays of furniture, the living room mockups, the bedrooms, the dining rooms—all of it. There was a sense of comfort there.

My whole family was involved in one way or another with the family business. My grandparents were there, uncles/aunts, and my dad was there, so it was just family. I loved the smell of the new tapestries, the wood, the curtains, and the carpet. It was new and full of possibilities. As a kid, I would play the game of "house" in these different furniture displays. I would imagine how the furniture would look in my house and it was—a place of love for me.

That night, when I arrived at the furniture store, I wanted to walk in and fade into the background of a living room set and sit in comfort and beauty for a few hours. I hoped to feel my grandma and my grandpa while I sat there. I wanted to remember light and love. I loved the way their home felt in all seasons of the year. I really needed to feel a sense of Christmas even though it was Valentine's. I came into the showroom and found a place tucked into the back, full of clean soft pillows, with a fresh farm feel, (think Joanna Gains from the TV show *Fixer-Upper*), complete with a rooster on the coffee table. I sat down on the couch, took a deep breath, and was still.

I thought a wave of emotion would overcome me. Nope. Nothing. I had about 45 minutes there in peace as I sat numbed out. My brain was so full of trauma and my belly was full of the result. I rubbed my baby bump and thought about raising all 5 children alone. I thought a wave of emotions would hit me then. No. Nothing.

Even though I was numb, no one had asked anything of me. No one had bothered me. No one knew I was there. I just took in the colors, the smell of the wood, and the carpet and just rested. But the quiet peaceful setting came to a crashing end when a salesman approached and asked me why I was there, and if I needed anything? I told him no. I was just looking. He kept pressing with comments like, "Please don't touch anything else."

This comment made me look down at my clothing. And I think for the first time I really looked at what I was wearing. These maternity clothes had been worn for 5 straight pregnancies over the past 8 years. They were "showing their age." I think he could see my worn clothing and that they had the look of poverty. Suddenly I heard the shadow in my head start to snicker. The salesman asked me to leave without exactly using those words. His face and body language revealed his judgement of me. I just smiled and nodded and walked away.

As I passed each showroom on the way out of the store, I could feel the other customers looking at me, even though their glances were quick. It was like I could hear their words from their mind: "Poor." "Unmarried." "Pregnant again." "No husband." Whether they said those words or not, it was what I could feel. Hecklers. They have all the judgment in the world and no skin in the game.

I smiled and nodded and walked away. A light snow was beginning to fall, and I soon found myself walking toward the van one hour earlier than I thought. I was leaving a place I thought I would find comfort in, but did not. It was disappointing. However, I was not going to pick up the kids yet.

As I stepped toward the curb and to my van, I looked down and found a quarter in the icy slush. I picked it up. As I was rising up, I found a few more quarters. Enough to make $1.25. I quickly opened the van and stepped up into the seat and slammed the door before I was covered in too much snow. I opened up my hand again and looked at the five quarters—$1.25! An idea struck me. I could go and get an ice cream. I could treat myself. Just me, and not have to share it with anyone!

I felt hope rising upward and felt that I had been given a gift. I drove through the snow with my wiper pushing off the flakes that were forming a small mound on the sides of the windshield. I drove to the famous ice cream shop. I was actually going to get a *Farr's Ice cream*! I remember getting a single scoop for $.75 just the year before. I had enough money to actually buy something that was just for me—something fun!

The smile that stretched across my face started to make the muscles ache. Apparently, I had not smiled much—especially as of late. With my face aching, I opened the van door move my belly out of the way, and slid down onto pavement with the heavy fat-flake rapidly falling snow and stepped over the curb onto the sidewalk toward the shop.

The windows of the shop were freshly decorated around the edges in icy patterns left by Jack Frost. Through the windows I could see that It was packed with customers, dates, sweethearts, and senior couples. They were all connected to each other through conversations and love.

As I grabbed hold of the icy metal and pulled there was a single chime of a bell, but no one seemed to notice. The gentle song *My Girl* was playing overhead. Everyone in that shop were so into their own lives that I felt like a ghost as I entered in. I wanted to grabbed my ice cream and float out before anyone noticed me.

My feet carried me toward the counter. There before me was the sweet smell of sugar and a rainbow of flavors: pinks, greens, colorful sprinkles, deep rich brown gooey, oranges, and purples. I could not believe the yummy goodness that was spread out before me and this time I was going to be able to order a cone: one scoop of strawberry on a sugar cone. "What can I get you, Miss?" I answered in a quiet voice, "One strawberry scoop on a sugar cone."

I watched the soda-jerk's hand hold the silver-scoop and slice into the soft pink cream and make a curl of pink to sit nicely on top of the toasted cone. This rich pink and chunky goodness was going to hit my lips and I could feel my mouth water. In the excitement of the moment, I reached for my change in my worn jeans. There in my hand were only three quarters... and a hole in the bottom of the pocket. As my finger slid across that frayed edges of the cotton fabric my hand went into the other pocket praying for a miracle. As my fingers touched the emptiness of that pocket, I knew that somewhere in the icy snowy depths of the sidewalk were two shiny quarters.

My heart sank. The money was gone. No! They can't be gone! I had just found them! Now they were lost. Suddenly I felt the Shadow come upon me, and all I heard was mocking laughter. "Stop!" I wanted to yell at it in my head. But it was too fast. Before I could say anything, the words came into my brain, "You don't deserve the ice cream anyway. How dare you think you can be more than you are."

I looked down at those three coins I had left—not enough! The soda jerk just looked at me like he didn't know what to do. He was holding the cone with the pink sweet chunky goodness on top, and I was short two quarters. Suddenly I noticed that all I could hear was the music overhead. There was no more conversation. No more talking of love from the customers. There was an awkward silence all but for the music. I could feel everyone looking at me. I could hear their thoughts penetrate me. I could feel the hecklers start up again both in my head and behind me. I dropped my hand that was reaching for the cone and said, "I lost my money. I don't have enough. I'm sorry to bother you."

As I turned away from the sweet colorful goodness, there was a couple who was looking at me and I slid my eyes down towards the floor. They caught my eye. I could feel her compassion but feel his glare. He was the one final heckler of the night. I stepped out the door and the last thing I remember was the song *My Girl* playing in the background.

I trudged through the snow to the van and got in. I quickly buckled, inserted the key, turned it over, and drove away. As each turn of the wheels went round through the slushy wet cold, I felt the tears pouring out of me. I felt the pain of the past five months cascade on me. I shut my eyes and felt the look of the couple again— her compassion and his glare. I was judged. This is the role of a Heckler—to be the outward judgement and confirmation of the Shame Shadow©. I'll never forget the look from that couple: the pity I felt from the woman and judgement I felt from him. The opposition was confirming. I was only good enough to receive a look of pity—an ice cream pity.

Do you see how the Hecklers have all the time and say in the world to get at you? They do and they will. In my book, *Pinpoints of Light: Escaping the Abyss of Abuse*, I share my story of how I found a way to gain financial freedom through work. Once I had my first paycheck in hand, I remember thinking, I will never again get to that point of being short $.50. I will work and save and get out and STAY out. Work gave me my way out of my first marriage that was filled with Domestic Violence (DV).

With my financial freedom from teaching, it was possible for me to never return to DV. However, sometimes in our freedom we become enslaved to something else because we are so grateful to escape our abyss of abuse.

I was so grateful for having my job that I unintentionally handed over power to a pair of Hecklers I worked with. I had no idea that I had done this, and they didn't rise up until I was in a place of absolute vulnerability. You see, desperation causes those who take advantage of other people a power that actually gives them control. I poured my heart and soul into my work because I was terrified of losing my job. Being a teacher got me away from the caged animal that was my ex and inadvertently I traded one abuser for another.

While working in my first teaching position, I was on a healing journey from the domestic abuse of my first marriage. My first few years while being a teacher, I was observing and doing my student teaching. That meant I was learning how to be a teacher in a classroom setting, completing my master's in special education degree, and learning from other leaders and teachers, but I was being paid. I was a sponge and was taking it all in, allowing my work to become a saving place for me.

Basically, I had never stopped my habit of pleasing, performing, or perfecting from my marriage, and I was pleasing, performing, and perfecting now for the school, especially the parents. I thought I was being service minded. I thought by working and sacrificing that I would feel that I was serving the students, parents, and staff. While that was true, the Hecklers saw this sacrifice as something to take advantage of. Remember, if you are a product of pleasing, performing, and perfecting, you feel that all of your worth—your light—gives to you by what you can produce. And then Hecklers can rule over you.

What I can see so clearly now is that my habits from my first marriage of *pleasing, performing and perfecting* were just transferred to work. I had left abuse and stepped into another form of it, but because this one paid me money, I took the abuse. I thought it was office politics. I was not going to move into any real position of leadership or get a raise in income, but they would be happy to tease me along, take my ideas, use me more through the contacts I had made, and take my intellectual property. I was being taken advantage of because I was loyal, and they knew it. They knew they had me on a chain because I had committed to staying there for as long as I had my children there.

A Spectrum of Judgement

How can one place go from your salvation to your destruction? The answer is when you trust in the arm of flesh and not fully in the Lord. When Hecklers attack, it can cost you your confidence, your worth and your light if you don't know how to weather the storm.

Field trips, homework, systems, new teaching, building from scratch, observing others at their craft, teaching to make a living, and sacrificing so much time to a school that gave me a new hope for life makes one very susceptible to Hecklers. This was me. I was loyal to a fault. I wanted to give back and stay committed to what I felt was helping and what I thought was right.

The gospel is easy to be loyal to because the Savior is perfect, forgiving, all knowing, and my Heavenly Father loves all of His children. For me, it is that simple. But, when I offer the same loyalty to something that is man-made, expecting the same treatment as my Savior and my Heavenly Father, well, shame on me.

If you are a leader with healthy leadership skills, you see an employee like this and make sure they know you are appreciative of their loyalty and work. These leaders protect, care, and love, but do not control you. Their love allows for production to continue because we feel relationally safe.

However, if you lead from a place of fear, then you are leading with micromanagement and control. You don't want to expose your weaknesses and so you demand the power and control to make sure everyone knows the rules. It can become a form of abuse depending on the actions that are happening.

For myself, I was so grateful for the job. I was grateful for what it provided for my family that I wanted to give all that I could: my time, my intellectual property, and service to Spectrum Academy. In return, I thought they would recognize it, praise it, and promote it.

No, that was not the case. After two years of work. I soon learned about the politics. No matter how loyal I was, they were taking what I was giving and expecting it to be there at all times. During my fifth-year teaching at Spectrum, my teaching career was threatened by a small group of parents. The head principal over both campuses did nothing to defend me. The assistant principal did everything in her limited power to try to support me. Ultimately, I felt like I was thrown under the bus, as it were. I thought I could ignore the actions of what happened during that year and keep running my classroom.

Well, here's the thing. Parents are a huge part of your work as a teacher and it takes just as much time to teach the parents what you are doing as it does their kids. When parents are upset about something you must address it and communicate clearly. I was given this opportunity on March 15, 2012. But really…. well, here is the story.

The Attack

March 15, 2012

Sitting in the principal's office, even as a teacher, your tummy will sometimes do a flip. I sat in a room with some parents, a mediator and our assistant principal. I knew that the parents had asked for a meeting. I did not know what was going to happen in the meeting or what they were so upset about. I had reached out by email and was given no response.

I thought that the meeting was held so that both sides could discuss the challenges that they felt, that we could address it, and try to find a pathway to help make things better. But what the complaints were really about I did not know.

It's a funny and awkward emotion right before we have a serious meeting with someone. It's like we are smile, nod our heads, share the pleasantries and then we walk through the office door, take our seats, throw away the social kindness and go for the kill! The assistant principal stated that the meeting was for the purpose to discuss both sides and that the mediator had been brought in to keep the meeting fair and unbiased.

Suddenly, the main parent pulled out a list of grievances that was signed petition style and she began to read them off one by one. This was the first introduction to the things I was going to be accused of. I was slammed and caught off guard by what the accusations were: 1) pushing students to complete academic work without taking into account their disability, 2) setting expectations that homework must be done in order to earn the field trip, 3) I use self-aggrandizing statements such as "The Admiral" and make the students call me that in the classroom, 4) leaving the classroom to attend IEP meetings for students who are in special education, to discuss goals as a team), 5) leaving early twice a month on Thursdays (15 minutes early) and finally, 6) I did not bother telling anyone that I was pregnant with my seventh child until my eighth month of pregnancy and they (the parents) had no idea they requested a teacher that would be out on maternity leave.

At the end of the paper she read, "These are reasons to ask for her resignation as a teacher for her deceit, and the pain she caused my child." She folded up and paper and smiled at me, waiting to pounce on any response that I gave her. I looked at the assistant principal and the mediator. Was she for real? These were the complaints? This was why I was called to this meeting? Honestly, the room was silent for a few moments.

In that silence, my brain was working on what she had just told me. 1) I make students do their work. 2) When they do the 15 minutes of homework each night that earns their way to the field trip. 3) I use *'self-aggrandizing statements.'* 4) *I have to attend Individual Education Plan Meetings for the 17 students that have IEP's in my classroom.* 5) I leave 15 minutes early on Thursdays twice a month—I'm driving one hour away so that I can get an American Sign Language lesson for my deaf daughter! I had cleared this with the school! 6) And the last one, I didn't tell anyone I was pregnant???"

My heart was so confused! Should I be laughing at this or take this seriously? I looked at the mediator and the assistant principal to see what their responses were. I say the mediator writing and the AP giving me that wincing, "just answer the accusations" look. My mind was trying to figure out if I would be fired. Would the school take the side of the parent? In that silence fear was gipping me—this was my only income. Afterward felt like a lifetime. I had no verbal response, but an emotional one. I fought to hold them back and be professional, but they had struck a nerve with everything I was trying to do in the classroom to teach their children accountability, responsibility, and respect. This became and emotional blender and the dam that holds back the tears broke. I went red faced. I was so embarrassed, but the tears were flowing down my face, and there was no stopping them.

This mom was NOT finished and went into a rant about how parents who had fought to get their children into my class were shocked and disappointed that I was not honest with them about my pregnancy. The personal attack about my pregnancy was the last straw. I looked at the school to defend me. No response. I sat there racking my brain! I had disclosed to my administration I was pregnant near the end of the school year last spring. I told them that baby would come in late September. I asked them to please work on the substitute situation over the summer so that we would be ready for the fall. That is the job of the administration!

This mother continued to complain that I did not share my pregnancy with the incoming parents and students who would be in my class in the fall of 2011.

She recounted her disappointment and anger on "back to school night" in mid-August. She said, "I fought to get my kid in your class. You never once disclosed your pregnancy to us as parents. Now, at back to school night you share that you are pregnant?" I searched the faces of the AP and the mediator. They encouraged me to answer this. I had no backing, no support in this. This was a personal matter. It was never "required" to disclose it to parents. I was so caught off guard. The mom was demanding that I should have revealed my pregnancy seven months ago so that she would not have been surprised at the back to school night. I tried to respond but the emotion was so tight and so thick across my throat that nothing came out.

The mom was not satisfied with my silence. She was complaining that "she would have to deal with a substitute" while I was on maternity leave. The mom then lit into complaining about my pregnancy, maternity leave, the substitute fiasco. As she spoke, again I turned to look at the AP and the mediator.

To give a quick background, in each classroom there is one teacher and one paraprofessional of two adults for 15 students with autism. Each grade level had two grade-level classes which meant two teachers and two paraprofessionals in every classroom. It takes two to run a class with students that have high special needs. Three weeks prior to me having my baby, my paraprofessional left for another job. So that meant I was running the class by myself. That was not a problem. Every day I would ask the team and the administration if they had found a replacement. "No one yet," was the reply. I was still 1 week away from having my baby and we as the 3rd 4th and 5th grade team were asked to put together a plan to share through all of the grades two people to fill my classroom. They were not going to hire anyone.

What the mom was talking about was actually true. 1) The school should have been responsible for finding my replacement, but they did not. 2) They asked me and the other fifth grade teacher to come up with a plan. (Basically, come up with a plan that involves *not hiring a substitute*). I was told to "make do with what you have." The charter school did not have enough money to hire a substitute to cover me for maternity leave. The end result was that the paraprofessional was pulled from the other 5th grade class to take over my class. 5th grade was down to one teacher and one paraprofessional for 32 students.

Was was the result? That decision was made on Friday September 9th. My baby was due September 17. But I went into labor and had my baby on September 10th. The teaching situation was setup to fail and boy did it! It was so bad that I ended up having to go back to work only after two weeks being home with my baby. The administration had no response to her. No apology to me. They had dropped the ball, but NEVER spoke up to that. Rather they looked at me and then she turned to me in that meeting waiting for me to respond to "why it was a disaster."

That was when the mediator *finally* stepped. The mediator acknowledged the fault of the school for not hiring anyone to replace April in the classroom. The mom and the principal got into that pretty deep. I felt a bit of relief that I she was using her anger on them and not on me for the moment. The school was in the wrong. It was not Apirl's job to find the replacement or create the employment plan for her maternity leave. The assistant principal owned that fault and the meeting quickly resumed to high tension focus back on me.

The mediator said, "These other grievances are very petty accusations." He went on to say that no one would be fired over them. The look on the mom's face was that of shock!

She was completely caught off guard by what he had said. The mom pounced on him and said, "April's expectations are too high for kids with autism! That forcing the kids to call me 'the Admiral' is uncalled for, and she is not teaching the kids because I was gone in meetings and leaving early on Thursdays!"

The mediator gave a calm response and explained that leaving twice a month 15 minutes early had been cleared by the school. He had a signed paper showing this. The mediator then faulted the school for not informing the parents of this change. No emails had been written to tell them. The mediator recommended that better communication between teachers, parents, and policies would be a huge key in resolving this conflict.

The mom was not satisfied and demanded to know what was more important: teaching her child or leaving each Thursday. That hit a spark and a flame of white-hot anger. It shot through me and I screamed back at her, "Because I need to learn sign language for my deaf daughter! She outranks your son all days of the year!"

That was my only outburst during the entire meeting, and the silence was thick following that explosion. The mediator was trying to regain control of the room where he could see the administration was not going to stand for me, and the parents wanted blood for nothing that was against my teaching contract.

The mediator began again, saying there were explanations for all of these things, but the parent was not going to listen and didn't care. She wanted me fired! The mediator stated again that no one would be fired. After a long moment of silence, the mediator stated that the parent needed to do one thing, and that was to restore my reputation. He told her she would need to go out and explain to the parents who had signed the petition to write an apology to me.

She was asked to send a text in that meeting to the group to state that April would not be fired, and they were to communicate their worries clearly directly to April and not to spread rumors around the school and community. (That letter and those texts never happened, by the way). The meeting ended with me still in tears, no defense of me from the administrators, and no victory for the parents, because I was not going to be fired.

The "heckling" I received on that day was out in the open and cut me down. Those Hecklers, really got to me because I was in such a pleasing, performing, and perfecting mindset, all I could feel was disbelief and guilt. I instantly started to think from her perspective and thought that she was probably right. She had expectations that I could not meet. She had built up in her mind that in my classroom she would find "the cure" for her son with Autism.

Facing that parent was like heading back into courtroom with my ex. I felt like I was facing my ex-husband in one of his manipulation-traps and all my skills dropped again. All I could do was cry because of the emotional ride. There was no real opportunity for me to explain my side, defend, or find a balance.

I discovered because of what happened in the parent meeting that I had not really changed. I was still *pleasing, perfecting, and performing.* I thought that if I was nice and loved others that my mistakes would be forgiven, and I would be given the benefit of the doubt. I thought that I could simply learn from my mistakes and change things on my own. I mean, I rarely complained about others, because that is contention, and so I just took it. I was not in a place to change my habits of the three P poison—not yet. However, I was now more aware of my weaknesses and with time (2017) I would learn how to make them my strengths.

Hecklers. I know you know who they are in your life. Write down the feelings that happens when you listen to them.

Or make a list of their names and find out if they still bring emotions up to the surface. This time is yours. Write and see how far you have come.

CHAPTER 8

Vulnerability Prism

What makes you vulnerable, make you beautiful.—Brene Brown

"And if men come unto me I will show unto them their weakness. I give unto men weakness that they may be humble; and my grace is sufficient for all men that humble themselves before me; for if they humble themselves before me, and have faith in me, then will I make weak things become strong unto them" (Ether 12:27).

Vulnerable and vulnerability. They are quite the buzzwords in today's society. We are encouraged to be more and more vulnerable in the workplace, at school, and on the stage of our lives, yet, for many of us, this is the *last* thing that we want to do. It is one thing to be vulnerable without any skills to know how to recover from it. I think it can even be a bit of peer pressure to "open up and be vulnerable" before we know that we can recover from it. Peers watch it happen and then many will leave you there, and where you thought it was a safe place to open up and try out your vulnerability, you soon find out you did it in front of Hecklers, not people who love you. (Remember Chapter 7—yes Hecklers are no good).

Moving on. We are given strengths and weaknesses which are the very crux of vulnerability. We can experience great fear and great faith, the deepest pain and the highest joy, and tangles of lies and the absolute truth. Being vulnerable is about our weaknesses and our strengths. I have weaknesses, but I can be brave enough to face them and take action to strengthen them in order to grow.

Why do we need to be vulnerable in order to grow? Because being vulnerable means you are opening yourself up to all sorts of opinions, critics, pain, and even deep truths. Who wants that? Well, honestly, many of us do when we see people who are *brave enough* to be vulnerable; we see that they are show-ing amazing *courage* and wish that we too could be like that. For example, in my mastermind group I am willing to ask the questions that leave me exposed as someone who doesn't know enough. That is a weakness that someone could attack and penetrate. Some have over the years. When that happens, I usually stay quiet, and end up missing more information, which keeps me weak instead of growing.

To be open and vulnerable is a big risk! What is the risk? We risk exposing our true self to others, wondering if we will be accepted or rejected. The fear of being accepted or rejected goes back to a primal nature that we have inside of us. It is connected to our very survival.

Humans are born into family units. As human beings, we are designed to be social creatures—meaning we need each other to survive the challenges of life. Think about it with a primal state of mind. If you were a caveman without a tribe or a group, what were your chances of survival? Not very high. Alone, you were vulnerable to the dangers of life. So, your natural instincts are to connect with others to be part of the tribe. As part of the tribe, you are going to contribute what you can, work hard, and never be vulnerable again, because being exposed like that could cost you your life.

How do you fight off the desire to stay safe by not exposing your weaknesses? How do you take down the wall and become vulnerable? You might not like the answer. We become vulnerable by making a choice to be so, and through that choice we are showing courage.

Showing courage is knowing that there will be pain, risk, and possibly failure involved, but *doing it anyway*. By looking at the choices given to you and thinking, *I want to jump to the next level* you must be willing to take the risk to learn and grow socially, mentally, emotionally, spiritually, and even physically—even when through that growing pain you are filled with doubt, second guess your decisions, want to quit, and you have so much fear.

Just as we choose to be vulnerable as our weaknesses are exposed, we start to learn. If we look at our failures as learning, then we can gain wisdom and perspective quickly that will lead us to rely on our strengths as our weakness become stronger! Soon, after enough exposure of life experiences in the Learning Zone (chapter 3), we are able to change our weaknesses into strengths. Now THAT is quite the payoff for being vulnerable.

Alright, not to completely change the subject, but we need to *geek* out for a few paragraphs. This chapter is called "Vulnerability Prism." It's time to learn the science of how prisms work. When **light passes through a prism** the **light** bends. When light is bent or refracted, the result is different colors that make up white **light** become separated. You will see a "rainbow" of colors as the light is bent in a prism. This happens because each color has a particular wavelength and each wavelength bends at a different angle; thus, we get color.

In the white light, we have all those colors. (Remember back in chapter two that we come from light!) We have a light inside of us! In order to know what we are "made of" so to speak, we will need to enter the Learning Zone. In the Learning Zone, we have the opportunity to hold the Vulnerability Prism which symbolically splits our internal light into a rainbow of colors. These symbolic colors represent both our strengths and weaknesses. We need both in order to know how to work, find the learning moments and change them to wins!

The challenge of holding the prism and looking at your colors is to find your strengths and weaknesses. They are all unique to you, and different from others. And where you will find a strength you will find an equal opposition. Just like we learned in Chapter 1—opposition in all things. The colors are there to help us see the diversity in what we need to learn and how we will respond and react to others.

Time to use your imagination. Close your eyes! Ok, picture this in your mind's eye. Imagine the scene: The Learning Zone stretches out in front of you with complexities and simplicities depending on what you need to learn. It feels wide and yet could be narrow. You see the Comfort Cage to the side and toward the back a little. And then suddenly, when you are ready, the prism rises up to meet you. The base and sides are clear. It captures your light and suddenly the light breaks into the colors that are meant for you.

Remember, in the Learning Zone, feeling the trials and challenges that are happening to you spiritually, emotionally, mentally or physically? It could be something like being called into your boss's office for a huge meeting or learning about a diagnosis from the doctor. These challenges that you are faced with come daily, sometimes hour by hour, and at other times months at a time. Nevertheless, you are in the Learning Zone.

Are you going to run toward the Comfort Cage out of fear when the trials happen? Or are you going to exercise the courage and make the decision to walk up to the Vulnerability Prism with all the courage you have and find out what you are made of? Are you ready to see both the strengths you have and the weaknesses? Are you willing to embrace both your strengths and weaknesses to go through the Learning Zone experience? Are you ready to see what happened when I held the Vulnerability Prism in the Learning Zone? I'll share two experiences and let's see where they take us? Here we go!

Public Speaking is...

In 2008, I was asked to speak at the Utah Autism Conference that was held in Ogden Utah. This was the start to my speaking career. I was terrified and yet I knew that this was right. I had been planning for months, practicing, building support and confidence. I had been asked to speak because of the work I was doing in my classroom with my students who were on the Autism Spectrum. The conference wanted me to share about why my classroom worked so smoothly. What were the tools I used for behavior and classroom management? I had one hour to share what I had developed, and my heart was ready this warm February morning.

Standing up in front with my laptop, my PowerPoint, my handouts, and my Post-It stickies. I grabbed the microphone and plunged in! That microphone was like the Vulnerability Prism. The rainbow of strengths and weaknesses seem to split out of me. I felt my stature shrink, my voice started to shake, and my legs started to tremble! But I looked at my audience. I looked at real people wanting help, who were there needing my message. I took hold of that microphone and began to speak truth. I could feel the right words form and start to tumble out of me. I shared research-based information and delivered it with light! From the hands that were writing the messages down, and the questions being asked, the power of the collective really took hold.

I knew I was still vulnerable in standing and delivering a message that might be accepted and rejected by others, but

I was willing to take that chance! I stood watching people writing down what I was saying. They were feeling something. They were connecting to my stories and to the solutions. They asked questions about the skill work I did and how I got my classroom to do what they did. I answered each question with confidence and with power until my time was up. I was hooked in doing this again and again.

I loved sharing my message even though the buildup was terrifying! Grabbing that microphone was going to reveal the good, the bad, and ugly—but it was worth it. That day transformed me, and I started submitting my name for speaking gigs in the summer while I continued to teach through the winter.

What are all the ways that we can be vulnerable throughout our life? What are the things that make you vulnerable? Some of you might even worry at the mention of that word that you are feeling sick in your stomach, or a stress headache is forming. It is tough stuff putting your TRUE self out there and getting slammed down, knocked down, and punched down. The trick is to keep getting back up while you are in the Learning Zone and keep going until we have learned what we needed to.

Holding the Vulnerability Prism is completely optional. You can dodge it while you are in the Learning Zone, and even run back to your Comfort Cage, but how does that work out for you? What happens after that? There are a certain percentage of us that stay there in the comfort cage and never come out again. Those people end up staying completely trapped in their world.

But there are others that, with trembling hands, reach out and grasp the Vulnerability Prism. Once they make that contact, as they see the colors of their strengths and weaknesses rainbow out, they can still make choices that help them to learn. There isn't failure—you simply learn what you can do differently next time. But don't be fooled. The Shame Shadow© is there trying to wrap you in doubt, fear, and ugliness. Turn away from it! Stay in the light! Look at your colors and see truth— because the truth sets your free.

Broken to the Bone

As I wrapped up my speaking at the Autism Conference, I was approached by someone I had never seen before. She looked to be a part of the conference and her expression was that of worry, concern, and panic! She asked me if my name was April and I told her yes. With that these next few sentences came pouring out of her mouth: "Please turn on your phone! There is a family emergency! They have been trying to reach you for an hour!"

That was all I remembered. It was a short conversation and I felt my feet turn in the direction of the exit. As I rounded the corner, I saw through the bank of windows that the weather forecast had changed from a warm February day to a blizzard! I stopped just before running out the door and grabbed my phone from my purse, turned it on, and immediately heard the bells, dings, and chimes of all the messages. With trembling hands pumped with anxiety, I held the phone up to my ear and listened to the message. "My name is Dr. Sanders. There has been an accident involving your son. Please contact me!"

I took the phone and frantically started dialing the number as my feet carried me out the door and into the wind whipped snow. My body was in auto gear racing to the van and I was trying to stay conscious in the moment to find out the information that I was going to hear on the other end of the receiver.

Words like, "near compound fracture, nerve bundle, possible damage, loss of strength, elbow, radius, humerus and emergency surgery" were being said to me. I unlocked the van, opened the door, threw my stuff in, slammed the door shut, and cranked over the key. I clicked my buckle and started praying as more questions were being fired off at me from the hospital: does he have allergies to meds, any prior surgeries, what are the effects of anesthesia, etc.

My tires left the dry parking garage and slammed into the slush and icy snow that was piling higher and higher by the minute. I could feel the wheel straighten and I headed my vehicle toward the interstate—toward the hospital! The 30-mile drive in blinding snow seem to fit the situation. I finally completed all the questions and the permission for my son to be in surgery as I carefully logged each snowy mile beneath me.

My heart was pounding. I had too many questions, and those led me to confusion because I had no answers, then it led me to stop, to remember my prayer and refocus on that. As I prayed for answers, it was like I suddenly grabbed the Vulnerability Prism again. I found myself vulnerable to the words of the shadow again. It started with the words of mother guilt: "not there for your kids, work priorities over family, getting a little too 'full of yourself', and not being a good mom." I was floored. Now?? Right now, in the midst of all of this I was going to have to do battle with the shadow.

I felt red hot anger flare up inside me and, if it were possible, it would have melted the snow off the freeway before me. I tilted my head upward and cried out to my Heavenly Father: "I can't do this by myself!" As soon as I said those words, I felt myself wanting to reach out and pull them back inside! Heavenly Father was listening, and this was going to be answered. I was in shock that the words had even surfaced! NO! I was still healing. I was still learning. I was supposed to stay single because I had messed up a first marriage! I mean REALLY?? Who was going to date an overworked, single mother of five children, three of whom were on the autism spectrum while she was getting her Master's in Special Education? Yeah right! What a catch!

Crunchy mile after snowy mile and swish and flick, swish and flick of the wipers were the only noise that filled the van after that. I was silenced. I had no words. I had no thoughts. All I could do was steer the van towards the hospital. The Shame Shadow© was silenced too. There was only a flicker of hope and a direction of light from the headlights through the snow to on.

Upon arriving at the hospital, I found the parking garage and ducked inside, found the closest parking spot and slammed it into park. As I gathered my purse, my phone, and pulled the key out of the starter, I was given one clear thought, "Do you trust me?" I hesitated for a fraction of a second and then hung my head and said, "Yes." Then I felt the response, "Then follow me." I took a deep breath and opened the door, jumped out, slammed it and ran through the parking garage toward the elevator that would lead me to my son.

Being vulnerable is not for the faint hearted. It is tough work to be exposed and to learn from that. But it is right. It is the refinement of growth in the Learning Zone that makes all of life possible. I was terrified that I was going to have to start dating and going through the ups and downs of relationships—talk about being vulnerable again——and for a while as I was going to have to take my time finding the right person—someone who loved me for me!

I know that you are dying to find out what had happened to my son. Well he suffered a compound fracture of his radius and humerus that required emergency surgery to save his arm. They did the surgery and my son's arm is fully functional.

How did it all happen? He was riding his bike during the "warm before the storm," meaning in February the weather can break a little and warm up with a southern wind, and then the slam of the north wind with the cold moisture hits. Well, because it was in the mid 50's in February he and his cousins were riding bikes at the skate park. They had been doing great for hours.

Soon it was time to go home and so the "final ride" was called out as a warning it was time to go. My son took one last dip into the skate bowl and as he peddled up the slope to get out he just didn't have enough push and gravity took hold of the bike, pulling it backward down the slope. He stuck out his arm to catch his fall. Then the handlebar did a karate chop as it hit his outstretched arm, causing the near compound fracture.

Moral of the story? When we put ourselves out there, we are vulnerable to external sources as well as to our internal sources. The battle is real. Show your courage. Being brave is what makes vulnerability amazing! The fight is real. The feelings are real, but the outcome of standing in the Learning Zone and holding the vulnerability prism is worth it. Courage is bravery. Show off what you love. Nothing is perfect, but there is perfection in practicing your courage! #vulnerableiscourage

Reflection:

When in your life did you risk being vulnerable? What was the risk that you took in doing it?

CHAPTER 9

Grounding

Get yourself grounded and you can navigate even the stormiest roads to peace.—Steve Goodier

"And now, my sons, remember, remember that it is upon the rock of our Redeemer, who is Christ, the Son of God, that ye must build your foundation; that when the devil shall send forth his mighty winds, yea, his shafts in the whirlwind, yea, when all his hail and his mighty storm shall beat upon you, it shall have no power over you to drag you down to the gulf of misery and endless wo, because of the rock upon which ye are built, which is a sure foundation, a foundation whereon if men build they cannot fall." (Helaman 5:12)

Grounding. What is it? This is a technique that has a huge variety of how to approach a situation and find yourself centered, balanced, or "down to earth" while "life" in the Learning Zone is happening. I call it grounding. This is not a new concept and grounding has many forms from meditation, to yoga, and even prayer. To understand how to keep yourself going and "grounded" while we are in the throes of the Learning Zone, we need to know the skills to ground ourselves while the storm of life is happening.

There are countless ways to use grounding, but for this book, I am going to teach you five. I use five different techniques: 1) Physical grounding, 2) breathing, 3) walk upon the earth, 4) flowing, and 5) music. I will discuss these techniques separately so that you can understand how each one works. When I need to be grounded sometimes, I will do a combination of the five in rapid succession, or just one depending on the situation and circumstance.

Physical grounding

Physical grounding is the process of focusing your senses. You are going to look closely at your surroundings and find all the physical earthly forms that you can find to use. You can shift your focus from people or events that are stressing you out and place that stress toward the physical things in the room: furniture, decorations, or lighting. Physical can also focus on sound. Such as water running in a fountain, or birds singing. Then engage your body in the most physical activity that you can: walking, running, weightlifting, resistance training, cycling, or swimming. Move to help you gain emotional calm and control again. This is grounding.

Perform breathing exercises

Breathing is a key component to grounding yourself. Thinking about breathing and taking it from the subconscious to the conscience is very meaningful. You are forced to think. Take a deep breath and count to one. Then hold it to two and exhale to three. Repeat again and again until you have your focus centered inside and you can shut out the sounds and the chaos and calm thoughts. If perilous thoughts come in your mind while you are breathing dismiss them immediately with your words and start breathing again. This method takes a lot of practice to work through because you are controlling your breathing and your thoughts at the same time. Be kind to yourself as you are practicing it and don't give up.

Walk directly upon the earth

This is the simplest form of getting grounded. If you are feeling emotionally overwhelmed, it is best to simply touch the earth by walking, sitting, feeling it. Stroll in the grass, in the dirt, in the sand of the beach. Feel the way that the elements connect with you between your toes and take the input pulling it up towards your light and find your balance naturally. In doing this, you are able to center yourself and find your light.

Enter a state of flow

Flow is something that happens when you have your mind ready to receive it. You can't force the flow, but you can give flow the opportunity to happen. Use other grounding methods prior to this one. You will know that you are in flow because you are so focused on the activity that it engulfs you and you lose track of time. This happens when you release your tension in the activity and focus in the moment of it. Following a session of flow, you will feel that you have found solutions and resolutions to what has been challenging you.

Listen to music

Music happens for us, to us, and inside us. The sounds, tune, harmony, melody, instruments, and voices happen in all cultures. Music is a language that crosses all barriers and therefore, it is universal. Music can stir intense emotions and bring you up from incredible lows. There is a balance as the pendulum swings from one side to the other and finds balance in the middle. Music helps you to relax and calm you. For me, this is the fastest way that I can find relaxation and emotional stability.

I combine these components of grounding: physical, breathing, standing on the earth or touching from the earth like the rock in my pocket, and think of music and have it playing if I'm lucky. (That's why it is so important to be exposed to all types of music so that you know what works for you and so you can keep a file of it in your head). The grounding that I use is the following, and is a technique that helps participants to take three deep breaths, state their name, touch something physical, and state three facts:

I am _____(name)

I can see _____

I can touch _____

I am Alive

I am _____ old

I am Light!

I am WORTH IT!

Getting Grounded

I was first formally introduced to this when I started counseling in college. I was going to have sixteen sessions with_____ who and the first three were all about building trust and connection. I was happy with how this was going, and I felt comfortable here. At first, I thought that it was very strange. I just didn't understand or buy into it quite frankly. At first it felt like trickery—like I was trying to call upon a power that I knew was there and I felt like it was all fake. I was definitely not raised with skills like this and so it felt very foreign.

My counselor tried having me start with making statements of who I was and where I was. I would roll my eyes and say:

"My name is April. I'm 19 years old. I can see a tree. I can touch the couch. I know that I am alive. I am worth fighting for." It was so strange to say those things that I already knew (or thought I knew). I had conversations in my head the whole time, *Didn't she understand my pain and what I needed? I do not need to say these things! I need to share my story!*

In saying those basics over and over again, I became irritated. I was getting very upset because I felt like I trusted her enough to share my story, but now we had shifted to this. My trust was leaving with this counselor, and I felt myself laying down bricks to wall everything back up. I figured I would just tell her what she wanted to hear, and that this was no longer about me but about her techniques and what she wanted. After all, I was a professional at pleasing, perfecting, and performing.

But everything shifted the next time I walked into the office. I heard music. It was gentle, but haunting, soft but penetrating, and suddenly connecting. I found myself gliding toward the chair to not disrupt the beauty of the music. Again, the music was powerful and was stirring up my emotions, but it was not loud or pounding. It had me in its grasps and when the solo violin sang out a piercing note, my spirit broke and the layers of bricks I was re-building came down in a tumbling crash. I noticed that my checks were wet with tears and my nose started to run as well. I was headed for a full-blown ugly cry.

As the dam of emotions broke open by the music in that office, so did my pain of the abuse in the neighbor's yard. The waves and layers of guilt, pain, not understanding how that could happen to me was washing over me like that of a cleansing pounding ocean. As I took in air I wanted to talk about my feelings, but I could not speak yet. The words were trapped by the emotion. But my head came alive with something new. I started to connect the pleasing, perfecting, and performing to the pain I had suffered all those years ago.

The music was still playing in the background. It was still and cleansing to me as my thoughts washing around in my head continued. Then suddenly, the violin carried a single note high into the scale then slid downward into the depths of a minor key and stayed there in a struggle gathering more and more notes towards it until it ascended again and resolving into a major key...the notes faded in the office and I was there, grounded.

My connection to that piece of music was the key. All the other grounding techniques of making statements felt false and unnatural, but the music grabbed me to my core. I needed to stay in this place of worth and release and resolve. My counselor looked my wet red face and then asked me one question, "What are you feeling?" And that was my starting place of where my healing all began.

Getting grounded is an important skill that will help you find some light while you are in Learning Zone. It's like you are empowered with a light cannon. You can light your pathway slicing through the darkness, keeping the shadow at bay before you and keeping your focus on the reality of the moment with the vision of the future in front of you.

Here are some questions to help you practice this skill:

Grounding: what technique will you need to try?

1) Physical Grounding
2) Breathing
3) Walk upon the earth
4) Flowing
5) Music

After experimenting to know what connects with you, write down your thoughts about how you feel when you use grounding.

SECTION 3

Recovering, Reflecting & Resting

CHAPTER 10

Recovery Road

We don't not learn from experience, we learn from reflection on experience. —John Dewey

"Take my yoke upon you, and learn of me; for I am meek and lowly in heart: and ye shall find rest unto your souls." (Matthew 11:29)

Recovery Road. What is this? You might think it's a place that you would find rest, but why is it a road and not like a bench, a chair, or even a bed to rest in? The answer to that is that these are places of reflection, recovery, and of rest, yet move with the ticking of time and so as each passing second clicks by you are gently moving, until you enter into another Recovery Road. RR's are the times when we leave the Learning Zone to walk and reflect on the events that occurred there. We reflect on what we learned—the growth, or the lack of growth that happened in the Learning Zone.

There are times during the recovery and reflection we will feel all the shame and pain of things. The sting of it will be there but the recovery time from an emotional "hit" will be less and less because it is reflection.

After each Learning Zone there is a Recovery Road. We are given this time of reflection and rest so that we are better prepared for the next Learning Zone because that is living life. If along the Recovery Road we feel that our reflection is shallow, we might not be getting the full benefit of the journey. We might be rushing on the Recovery Road and not really giving ourselves time needed to prepare ourselves for the next Learning Zone. There are times where our reflection is deep, meaningful and refreshing. There are always choices in life and what we choose to do on the RR helps us to understand more of what we need in the next zone.

Now a word of caution: If you are not in a healthy state of mind while you are on the symbolic Recovery Road, your reflection will find all the flaws that happened there, and the Shame Shadow© can raise its head and start to whisper to you again. It will block what you learned. You will not turn to the light. You will be in the shadow and stay in the darkness of its grasp. You'll find yourself being pulled back to the comfort cage if you aren't careful, and back into another Learning Zone in that state of mind.

However, if you are willing to turn from the shadow and reflect on the recovery road about your growth—about what you learned, you will find your light. In the light, you will take time recovering, resting, and reflecting on your wins and learns. You will find the growth and it will become a part of who you are. This will add to your oil that fuels your light. As you age, you will be less likely to repeat those patterns of behavior and bad choices, but remember with mercy the feeling of that trial so that you are not trapped in the guilt of anything, but that you are liberated from making that same mistake again.

The word Recovery really covers three areas: physical, spiritual, and mental. When I think of the word *rest*, I think about how our physical bodies heal. They need sleep, nutrition, care, and compassion. When I think about the word reflection, I think about how our spirits heal, they need time to recall and think. Spirituality also needs mercy, and an opportunity to repent. We then need to forgive, and to extend grace. When I think about mental health I think about reflection. I think about my thinking, my emotions, my behaviors, my positive light that I focus in on to scorch the Shame Shadow© to lessen its power and keep me turned toward the light.

The challenge with the Recovery Road is, as we leave the Learning Zone in an unhealthy state of mind, we might just invite the Shame Shadow© to hold our hand and share all the negativity: flaws, what you did wrong, your mistakes, your lack of any good, your shame, and your darkness. When doing this deep reflection in darkness your ability to recover is like taking a placebo pill verses taking real medicine for the infection. The infection of darkness when you are turned and looking at the shadow, won't help you recover from anything, and when you return to the Learning Zone you will become weak.

On the other hand, when you are facing the light, your recovery, rest, and reflection will be amazing. With light you can see the truth. You can see the answers. You can gain perspective. You can be enlightened, empowered, and encouraged! That gives you rest and restoration.

Sharing deep reflection of two of my recovery roads, leaves me feeling very vulnerable. However, that too is part of the growth, right? There is beauty in that vulnerability. In our recovery road, we get to reflect on everything. I want to share with you two of my personal experiences: one that led me to darkness and one that led me to light. Remember what I said at the beginning of this chapter? If we walk on the recovery road in an unhealthy state of mind, we may not find full recovery or rest, and may have to go back into the Learning Zone and try again.

Free Falling

I remember leaning my head against the double paned pressurized glass of the airplane with my breath clouding the view through the glass and feeling the coldness of it as it pressed against my forehead. My tears ran from my eyes down onto the rounded windowpane. There were no words, just hours of silent crying as the heavy metal wings rose up into the atmosphere, bringing me home.

My flight home from that national tumbling competition was filled with hours of silent sulking, crying and feeling like a failure. The dark Shame Shadow© was right there to feed into the loss of my competition, which confirmed my failure again and again. My tumbling, my ability to win, my value; they were all tied to what I could produce. This national championship defined who I was, what my value was—or so I was led to believe from the Shame Shadow©.

When I crashed at the National Power Tumbling Championship in Baton Rouge Louisiana, I didn't understand how to handle the feelings of losing—of not being a winner. Did this mean that I was any less April, or of the person I thought I was?

The terrifying reality that hit me was that I had based my self-worth on what I could produce. If I couldn't produce another championship, then what was my value? This was a huge cause of my tears. From that fall I had disappointed myself, my family, and my friends. I don't fall. I don't always win, but I don't fall. As air mile after air mile zoomed beneath me I settled into accepting the words in my mind that I was done… no longer worthy of doing tumbling.

Needless to say, I never returned to competition. I had questions that banged around in my head for years: are you sure you can do it? You need a long time to figure things out. Maybe you're not good enough to compete at this level so why don't you find a place that is more accepting." All this did was turn me toward more doubt and worthlessness. I gave the Shame Shadow© way too much power at this time because I hadn't dealt with the pain of my earlier childhood; and so pleasing, perfecting, and performing was running rampant in my thoughts.

I let that moment define me as a loser at tumbling and probably most of everything else that I did—more doubt, more worthlessness. I reflected on those words on the recovery road: looser, can't, pathetic, lazy, failure, too much, not enough, and the worst, fallen angel. I would just have to pour my focus into something else because it was too painful and too hard to try to face that failure again.

My worth—my ability to flip, to fly, to do something different than anyone else in my family, for me, was over. I had no control over my ability to flip, twist, or land. I had no control of my work or my practice because if I fell again, I would fail again! There was no longer any control. No control and nothing I could do. I was dependent on a judge to tell me of my worth. I needed to find control! I needed to control something, anything. I was spinning and spinning with no landing in sight.

This competition happened in July 1991. One month later I would begin my senior year in high school. I had been competing for over 9 years, and now I had walked away. I left the years of competition, practice, and my investment because I had failed! And I was convinced that I needed to control something in my life after failing. I needed to find myself again. I needed to find something I could produce, somewhere I could find my worth.

On this recovery road, I found myself facing a fork in the road. The path split before me. My brain was racing to make a decision—it wanted to make the right choice. Fear gripped me again and sent me spinning into a world of decisions: *Go left! No! Go right! No, left! No—right!* My head was shifting from left to right trying to make a decision. It just kept repeating it over and over and over while I was trying to walk on this Recovery Road. Then suddenly, the switching stopped! The silence entered into my head, and I stepped toward the left. I heard the Shame Shadow© congratulate me.

I was committed to walk this path because I had been convinced that that is what my worth was, even though the Shame Shadow© was the one laughing and congratulating me. All I could feel was that I would finally have a sense of control! I would have a sense of pride! I would change the way that I felt. I would control my life, fully. What did I try to control? I started with the one thing that I needed every day—food!

I left my reflection/recovery road and entered into another Learning Zone. This Learning Zone was my Anorexia Abyss. It would take me years to leave it alone. So you see, some Recovery Roads lead to true healing and others lead to more things to learn.

Transcending Truth

At age 20, after my freshman year of college was completed, I had an opportunity to travel to the UK and hike in three countries. My Recovery Road as I climbed the mountains in England, Scotland, and Wales was very different from my Recovery Road and reflection after crashing at nationals. I was older, I was wiser, and I had overcome my bad relationship with my first boyfriend. I was out of my anorexia. I regained a sense of understanding of myself through counseling. But I still was afraid. This fear was cultural, but it was also fed by religion. What was the fear that I was facing? I thought I would be alone forever and would never get married. So, I entered a recovery road reflecting on getting married.

I felt that I had learned so much and I was finally better from my crazy was of thinking thanks to counseling. I felt that this would be a perfect time to get ready for marriage. The problem was that I had wasn't dating anyone. I didn't even say hi to any guys on campus. I just didn't really know how to date. Minor troubles, right? I know, y'all can laugh out loud. I am as I'm writing this again.

What do you do if you don't have anyone to date or get married to? Well, you start showing up to the parties, to church gatherings, to dances, and you start the ripples that you are available. It took a little bit of time, but after working the single rounds at all church functions and dances, I was newly engaged to Peter—after only two months of trying!

Although our meeting and dating were swift, the engagement was like the movies! Peter was caring and romantic. He was very attentive. He was brilliant. He was kind of annoying, but I was so ready to get married, settle down, and start my life that I figured I would just get over that.

During the whirlwind dating and engagement, I forgot that I had signed up in the fall of that school year to go on an internship/study abroad in the UK for about seven weeks. Even though I was newly engaged to Peter, I explained that I would be back and to not worry. He was worried. He was pretty freaked out that I was headed off without him and that I was - so casual about it. I saw it as just a trip. (This demonstrates how immature and not ready I was for a lifetime commitment like marriage).

I knew that being physically separated from Peter was going to be fine with me because I knew that he was devoted to me. Feeling secure in this, going to the UK for seven weeks was going to be the cherry on top! I knew I would enjoy hiking those hills. I knew that it was not a physical endurance challenge for me, but it would be a time of great reflection. I would find all that I needed to be confirmed true, would be—my answer to marry Peter. I was confident that in his absence, I would find a way to love *him*, and not just the idea of getting married.

Well, recovery roads are very different from the Learning Zones. The piece of reflection, recovery and healing comes at a price. You still have to decide if you want to heal or stay in the pain of life. To give you even deeper background, I had left a very serious relationship only months before, and now in my freshman year of college, had started counseling for my anorexia and depression (chapter 9).

I knew I needed to get away to take that break and test my love for Peter. After all, I was newly engaged! This was a lot to try to figure out. I declared myself an English major because I enjoyed writing. I figured this would be a way for me to actually finished my degree. The trip would serve all these purposes and more. Little did I know how much more it would do.

Ben Nevis Reflection leading to Honesty

Crunch, Crunch, Crunch, Crunch came the sound of my hiking boots on the crushed rock on the side of Ben Nevis. The chilly dampness in the air was real and soon our pathway was covered with thick white fog. I pulled out my jacket and hat, watching as my pathway disappeared in front of my eyes. I was in Scotland for a seven-week study abroad with the University. It was July 24, 1993.

Even though my view of the tallest mountain in the UK had been swallowed up in the storm, my goal that day was still to climb to the top of Ben Nevis. I took in a deep breath and turned toward the direction of the summit. I began the same rhythmic stepping towards my goal, and with each step of my short frame, I began to reflect on the past two years of my life.

What had I learned? There had been successes, deep failures, dark depression, a spark of hope, then a grip of fear. That fear was why I was on the mountain that day. I was afraid to have an honest conversation with myself. I was terrified of admitting the truth to myself. Terrified. If I admitted this truth then I would be laughed at, teased, mocked, humiliated, but more importantly, this truth would change the course of my life—I felt it would change it in the direction toward absolute failure. That was what I was so afraid of.

My hike on this mountain was a Recovery Road. It was like I could see a "movie" being replayed in my head and in my heart. I was reliving with each step the fear and need to control everything with my anorexia. The Shame Shadow© was NOT there (or at least I was not focused on him). It was just my heart and mind reflecting on why I had to control food—because I felt so out of control.

With more steps on the mountain, I was feeling the pain of breaking up with my high school sweetheart, but I was not ashamed. No shadow was following me. Step, crunch, step, crunch. I had no feeling of failure about receiving counseling for my depression. I had no guilt because of my anorexia or my breakup with my boyfriend. The recovery road started to become a checklist of all the things I had overcome! The mountain was this place of reflection. More miles. More crunching and stepping under my feet. More reflecting on my wins—my light!

Then suddenly, my fear of being alone or not being married began to surface as I climbed higher and higher into the dense fog. These thoughts were real, but I was not terrified. I was shocked! I thought for sure they would overwhelm me. No, it was more like I was watching a movie and not reliving it. This was TRUE reflection.

The fear that drove me to start dating again was now being reflected on. Step crunch, step crunch. I was engaged to Peter. He was nice, smart, and simple. He was poor, but that would change after college because he was a science major studying physics. But there was something about Peter...

Peter annoyed me a little bit because he was over-attentive. What? He paid attention to you and you didn't know how to handle that? Yes. I know it sounds weird, but that was something I was NOT used to. I was more used to trying to get the guy's attention. Trying to ALWAYS please, perform and perfect; but with Peter he was there. Ready. Almost too ready all the time. I knew that he would be there when I returned.

My feet were pacing up the trail and it felt good. My mind began to fall into a trance with the stepping sounds of my boots hitting the pathway. I was reflecting on and seeing all my positive light. I could see what I had accomplished during my freshman year, even though the pain of that year was something I never wanted to repeat.

As my mind kept reflecting on things of the past, my body that was hiking Ben Nevis was keeping up the pace with the group. The green emerald hills were scarred with lines of cliffs and rocks. There soon began an intense ascent as our feet started to gain elevation. The incline increased and the group started to separate. We were grouped in pockets of fours and threes. Conversations started to fade with the elevation, and swiftly, a white dense fog crept in and collect all around us, sopping the mountain.

As the thickness of the fog grew, the clarity in my mind started to fade. Even though my feet kept working their way up the mountain, I began to fall into a fog and soon my mind bumped into a dark figure. The Shame Shadow©. It had not been there during all that reflection. Why would I run into it here? With the fog physically around me, my mind was also losing light and soon I was facing the dark shadow. I knew this darkness. This was what I had been fighting my whole

Freshman year. But I kept thinking to myself, I was on a recovery road! I was not in a Learning Zone—why was it here??

The blackness of my mind surrounded me and words— dark heavy words started to echo in my head. I tried to shake my mind and hold onto something that was here physically. I stopped my pace and shrugged off my pack in an effort to distract myself, but the words were still coming in. "Failure, dishonest, liar…" I shook my head and physically reached for some food and water. I put that back in my pack and pulled out my jacket. The words faded.

Getting out of my head and physically changing things to food and water was working. Stay in the present. Ground yourself, I commanded myself. I zipped up everything and slid my pack back on. I began my pace and started going steadily. The rhythm was back.

I was reflecting again, when suddenly and symbolically like I had stepped on a tripwire, a bomb of pain went off in my heart! The pain was from my lowest low of being utterly alone! It started to envelop me. In my pain, I could hear the words, "alone…forever!" I wanted to shout out, but I couldn't. I just kept walking. I tried to ground myself once more. Step, crunch, step, crunch. Stay on the path!

"Alone…forever," it whispered again! I found myself gripping my engagement ring tighter and tighter! *No!* I screamed in my head. I would not be alone. I tried to put the image of my fiancé in my head. I needed proof that I was not alone. I was engaged. I would be with Peter. I forced the image up in my head.

The image came in sharp and clear and then faded out into the fog. I tried to keep the image of my fiancé up in my conscious mind but was unsuccessful. This time in sheer terror, I screamed out through the fog, "I will not be alone!" Why could my mind not see his face? Suddenly, it was like a beam of light sliced through my foggy darkness. I heard these words in my head, "you must be honest with yourself!"

My feet took two more steps: Crunch step, crunch step—I stood there breathing deeply. I was lost—physically lost in a foreign country and on a mountain with no map! In my pain, my desire to get away from the shadow, the mountain had turned on me. Suddenly I went from a clear path to scramble on the loose shell and pebbles. I don't remember this being part of the route I thought to myself. I froze right there. I looked all around me in a 360 circle and I was utterly alone. I could hear no one. The fog was even thicker, if that was possible. The voice in my head was just an echo now, and I was alone!

I shrugged off my pack and rummaged to find the map. I unfolded it, trying to get my bearings; to know where I could possibly be. After some time of frantic searching, with my eyes scanning the map and thinking I knew where I was, it hit me that I was near the edge of the cliff. I was so lost in my reflection, my pain, and my fear that I was now in physical danger, facing the reality that I could literally walk off a cliff.

I didn't know what to do. I started to reach around me for my backpack I had placed on the ground, and my feet started to slide on the loose shell. So I stopped. I finally started to pray. I prayed with all the fervor I could muster on the side of Ben Nevis. I felt like my prayer was trapped with the thick fog and it would never reach upward. I shut my eyes tighter and quieted my soul! What could I do? I started to take deep breaths and dig my feet deep in the shell. I finally cried out, "I am afraid! I need your help!"

It seemed to penetrate through the heavy wetness, and suddenly a breeze came out from behind me and started to lighten the fog. I could see about 25 feet in front of me! I was four feet away from walking off the cliff. With my heart thumping in my chest, I turned back and retraced my steps towards what I hoped was the trail. It was a scramble through the shell until I found the solid pathway. As my feet touched the path I knelt in prayer and thanked my Heavenly Father.

On my knees and in intense prayer, the reflection from the past two years came crashing in on me. I was overcome by an emotional wave that slammed me into the queen of all ugly cries. I reflected on all my pain and the choices that led me there: 1) my anorexia, 2) breaking up with my boyfriend, 3) starting college, 4) finding myself in the darkness of depression, and 5) rushing to get engaged all out of fear.

On the side of the mountain on my knees truly praying and feeling connected, I faced my fear of being alone and came to a decision point. I admitted to myself quietly at first and then out loud that I was only in love with the idea of getting married—so I wouldn't be alone. I was not really in love with Peter. Those words hung in the air with the fog and seemed to stare at me. That truth did not fade! I was using him to fulfill my idea of dating and getting married. I was not being truthful to him. That's why I could not recall his face. That's why I would have to tell myself to think of him. That's why I did not deserve him.

He was a sweet, hard-working, faith-filled and dedicated man and he deserved someone who was devoted to him. I was terrified of being alone, but that was not fair to Peter. I feel that marriage is a commitment for eternity. I was not looking at this in that mind set. I was simply running from my shame, fear, and pain. I was hoping that this comfort cage of getting married would help me to not be alone. What was I thinking? I was thinking that the comfort cage would be better than really being in love with all the risks and ups and downs that happen? STOP! I must be honest with myself—and NOW!

My hand reached over and touched the ring on my finger, and my eyes shot open. I knew, in that reflection, that I must break off my engagement. I could not lead Peter into a lie and a commitment of marriage and not even be in love with him.

It was all my fault. I would be entering into a marriage out of fear and my self-worth and light were barely flickering. If any trial would come upon my marriage, I'm sure that I would break and that would bring the marriage down. I slowly got off my numb knees and stood to face more fog. I knew I had to make an international phone call as soon as I was off the mountain. It would only be fair to Peter.

As soon as that realization happened, I found myself walking again. My feet seemed to mechanically start climbing up the trail. With all those steps, I soon found my group again, and together we made it to the summit. I never saw the view, for the fog still clouded over the mountain, but I felt the joy of making it to the top. As we turned to make our descent, my heart was filled with light. I knew I had made the right choice. I had overcome so much of my fear through this reflection, that with each step I was closer to telling Peter the truth and setting him free from me and all my problems. I was still healing. I still needed time. This recovery road lead me to light.

My seven weeks in the UK was spent studying transcendentalism: it taught that divinity pervades all nature and humanity. In the nature of the UK hiking, walking, and scaling the mountains, the lake district, and any elevation was emerald green, I was in an emotional, mental, and spiritual Recovery Road. This was my time to reflect, regain myself and recover from all that pain.

I placed a phone call to Peter and told him everything. It was not well received. I crushed him. I was honest and so the truth prevailed, but the emotions and tears led to a dark night. The mountains in England, Scotland, and Wales, however, saved me. The Recovery Road gave me deep reflection and healing. I knew that I would be ready to go back to my next Learning Zone upon returning to the states.

How do you use a Recovery Road? Remember that it is for reflection, recovery, and of rest.

Here is the exercise:

Please write down the Recovery Roads you have had in your lifetime. Listing and identifying them are powerful exercises. Be patient with yourself but list them by giving them a title or a description.

CHAPTER 11

Love! After All,
Life is a Love Story.

We need the Darkest Night to see the Brightest Stars!—April
Tribe Giauque

"As I have loved you, love one another. By this shall
men know ye are my disciples, if ye hath loved, one to
another." (John 13:34-35)

Light, love, and lack: when we have light, we have love,
therefore, we lack nothing. But, when we lack, we have
neither light nor love. We are programed to want to be loved
and accepted. It is a huge part of what makes us connected to
each other. Heavenly Father designed us to be in families, to
love one another, and to make choices. When we experience
lack in our heart, abilities, or words, it means we may not have
the skill, the knowledge, or the ability yet in doing, thinking,

or being something. The lack gives us drive to want to find answers, or it can make us feel weak and scared.

Lack is very important to know that something is missing. There is a drive or a nudge to try to find something. That search leads us to find love and light. Our search gives us an opportunity to learn something new while we are in the Learning Zone. We can get anxious about what we are experiencing, or *not* feel like we are in control, and to run to the Comfort Cage. In the CC we think that comfort is there and when we find that it is not, we can listen or not listen to the Shame Shadow© and step back into the Learning Zone.

Once we are back in the LZ we are smarter and will pick up the battle again, but this time use Grounding to make it through the learns, fails, and wins. Finally, we then have the opportunity to reflect on what was learned in the LZ. Remember, all we lacked but now look back on all we have gained, and we are better prepared to fill in the gap.

Opposition in all things—that is why we will lack in this life. Heavenly Father loves us enough to give us agency to make choices. Part of trying to find light and love is done through our lack. It drives us to know more and fill in our gap, caused by the lack and then we can experience faith, light, and love!

Since this chapter is about love, I thought I would share a talk I gave in church last Christmas. *Love is the Savior.*

How do you spell Christmas? L-O-V-E.

L - Light. The light in the heart of a mother. The light to others. The light of the star. The light of the eyes of a newborn babe. The Savior is the light and life of the world.

O - Openness of our hearts. The openness of how we give our substance to others. The openness of the love of the Savior and how he gave to all he met and served.

V Victory. Victory over the Shame Shadow©. Victory over illness. Victory over sickness, mental illness, abuse, heartache, pain, cancer, tragedy, accidents, wars, hurt hearts, loneliness, and death.

E - Everyone can Partake. Everyone can feel the hope that His light brings. Everyone can share and bask in that light which is the ultimate love, for the Savior's love is for all!

Following such positivity there will usually be doubt. The questions that begin because of doubt are: **Can we**:

Love enough to do, learn, and progress?

Love enough to fight hard, and daily, against negativity and the Shame Shadow©?

Love enough to think of others first?

Love enough to repent?

Love enough to forgive others?

Love enough to forgive ourselves?

Love enough to be patient with ourselves?

Love enough to be kind to ourselves?

Love enough to not kick ourselves when we are down?

Love the Lord enough to trust His atonement for us?

Love enough to fill ourselves with light?

Love enough to fuel our light?

Love enough to amplify our light to all so that we can become a beacon of light?

The answer to all of these questions is yes we can but only with time and with help. Now whether you believe in a higher power or not, that is fine. For me I searched for this love for years! 43 years to be exact. But...I found it! How I found it still amazes me.

Face to Face with Love

Nineteen, twenty, twenty-one. *There*, I think. *That is the last laundry load of the week.* The empty basket gently swings in my hand as my eye scales the mountain of clothes that I have dumped in the living room. Twenty-one loads per week, every week like clockwork. I take a deep breath and look at the clock. It's 7:30 in the evening on the Sabbath day. I defiantly have my "ox in the mire" on this one so I set my computer on the table and turn on a "Face to Face" recording to help me along as I folded and separated the mountain of laundry.

As the program unfolds, I find myself listening with an open heart to the words that 10 people from my favorite comedy-sketch show are saying. They are sharing testimony about Christ: His Atonement, His power to heal, and His love for all.

My hands are pressing on the soft blue blanket of my 2-year-old and suddenly my ears hear this, "As soon as my little boy was born, I was overwhelmed by a feeling of love! He hadn't even done anything, but I was overcome with love for him and I knew suddenly how Heavenly Father loves us. He didn't have to do anything but just be..."

I found the blanket wet and my tears were falling on it. I was suddenly transported back nine different times as I delivered each of my children, understanding that love—that bond—that intensity of love for this tiny helpless creature. I had known that before, but the difference this time it was the phrase, "He hadn't even done anything."

My folding hands stopped, and as I sat in the Spirit of that moment, I understood that I no longer had to *"please, perform, or perfect"* to find Heavenly Father's love. I no longer needed to *prove myself* to Him or to anyone for their love. I finally understood at that moment with the mountain of laundry—the everyday type of task—that I was loved because I had life! I was alive. I was God's child.

I was His. I was from His light therefore I was love and I was loved! I was enveloped in a sweeping peace. My eyes seemed to release the emotions of 43 years' worth of being free! The Shame Shadow© was deep in the dark. It tried to speak but it was strangled off by the power of light coming from within me. He was silenced! He was behind me. He was not in charge. I had fully tuned into the Savior, the Spirit, and my Heavenly Father!

My hands held that blue blanket with the pies of laundry still around me but my heart was focused on this truth I was feeling. The light, the peace, the burning understanding that I was loved because I was His! I had to say it again and again and again. "I am loved! I am loved! I didn't have to do anything! I am loved! I am worthy of the love! I am forever loved! I am deeply loved. I am important to Him. He knows me! He knows my heart. I don't have to prove anything to anyone! I know I am loved! I am His! I am loved!

The flashing images of my life that went across my heart and my head and were burned into me by the Spirit. It was an out-of-body experience to understand it all. I was fixated in a peace and so much light that I felt my chest nearly start to burn and glow. This feeling of love, peace, and power encompassed every inch of my body. It seemed to be the cleansing burn of the Holy Spirit confirming to me that Jesus and Heavenly Father knew me. I was not just acceptable to Him, but I was KNOWN of Him! Little old me. They knew my heat, the desires of it.

The deep tender mercies that I never share with anyone, they seemed to open and flash before me! They welled up and recalled to my mind all the gifts and blessing I have in my life. All of it was coming because I was worth it. I am God's. I am a child of God. I am His! I am loved because I have life!

This life changing moment lasted for 20 minutes. I had peace! I had no interruptions from children. I had peace. I was in the moment! Then slowly the intensity began to gently fade, but it didn't leave. The gentle glow remained. Just for a moment I had a thought to "look behind me." I looked inwardly behind me at the shadow. It was there. But it was silenced.

I innately began to understand that I had had the power all along to make this choice to listen to it or not. It dawned on me that the blackness would always be there, it was there to help me to know the opposition in all things. BUT I had a choice. I can keep myself turned towards the light. I can keep light within me. I have light within me! I am made of God's light! I am worthy of it therefore it NEVER goes away. I just have to choose Light or Darkness. I had I needed to feel that darkness for so many years until I could finally understand that I was light! I always had it with me.

At 43 years-old I walked *out of darkness*! I knew it was always back there, but I finally understood how to walk out of it!

This is a quote by often attributed to Mother Teresa:

"If you are kind, people may accuse you of selfish, ulterior motives.

Be kind anyway.

What you spend years building, someone could destroy overnight.

Build anyway. he good you do today, people will often forget tomorrow.

Do good anyway.

Give the world the best you have, and it may never be enough.

Give the world the best you've got anyway.

You see, in the final analysis, it is between you and your God … anyway."

Why do some people inherently do good? Why do they care for others outside of themselves? Why do they see a need and then have a desire to fix or fulfill it? Because of love and because of light! They know their worth and their light and they are ready to serve and love others. I have performed the act of love for others and did things to please others, but always with a "condition" attached to it. But since my Face to Face and finding that I was love because I was alive, things changed.

Feeling that you have to have perfect love or be absolutely worthy of love before you can be loved is the lie of the Shame Shadow©. Remember the pleasing, perfecting, performing act that the Shame Shadow© pushes on us? Our ability to love others is like this: love is action not perfection so don't despair—act!

We can all get to that point of despair, but don't let it take over. Make the choice to work through it and see what can happen. We all have a light inside of us, but we also have the natural man inside of us. Remember in chapter 1, we talked about opposition in all things and that there must be an equal and opposite for good and bad in order for us to make choices? When we chose light and love over the natural man, the negativity, and/or the Shame Shadow© we are in His love!

Ok—are you ready for one more light/star geek out session? YES! Me too! What do you know about black holes in our universe? They are the remnants of a star that has collapsed, right? Right, but after 15 years of research, scientists have discovered something that is mind-blowing. There is a type of black holes called "Supermassive's," that actually are the key that allows galaxies to function. According to the latest research, astrophysicists are coming to realize that Supermassive black holes just might be integral to the structure of the universe—and our very existence.

You see, the Hubble Telescope captured amazing pictures of the Milky Way Galaxy. Scientists spent the last 15 years mapping out the stars and light signatures of the galaxy with the help of computers. They mapped the stars and how they orbit, until they built up a "library of how stars orbit in a galaxy."

Now for the scientists, success was obtained when the model—everything that they mapped with computers—matched the observations taken with the Hubble Space Telescope.

Time and time again as the astrophysicists were creating models of everything they had mapped out in the galaxy, the computer model *never* turned out like the picture from the Hubble. Why? Scientist started asking themselves what they were missing. Why was the galaxy not rotating like from the Hubble? No answers. The scientists were stumped!

Then, as they analyzed what they were looking at a little closer, the astrophysicists wondered what would happen if they added a Supermassive blackhole in the center of their model on the computer. As soon as they added the Supermassive blackhole, the galaxies finally matched the observations from the Hubble observations. So what? Who cares? For our purposes it is just one more point of proof that we will have opposition in all things. Remember that with opposition in all things it allows you to make choices.

Why are we talking about galaxies, supermassive blackholes, choices, and love? Because in order for love to truly reign, we need to have the agency to make the choices. Just like with the galaxies, in order for them to truly spin and keep the laws of physics in harmony we need supermassive blackholes—all that light with all that darkness. We need choices! Heavenly Father loves us enough for us to be given opposition in all things so that we may choose for ourselves whether we will follow light or be swallowed up in darkness.

How I have responded to all the choices, both the lack and the light, in my life over the years has given me wisdom. What I discovered was that it is a process, a journey, and it takes time. I've finally accepted that. I used to think about love as very two dimensional: you either had it or you didn't.

That you either kept the love or lost the love. That if you made mistakes your "ranking" fell, or if you didn't do it in a way someone else wanted you to then you were at fault—more of what you lack!

I now know that I can't control love—how others give it to me, but that I can get better at love if I love others first and try to make connections and give it first. If I reach out, the love that is reciprocated is truer and firmer. But I also have to remember that love might not be reciprocated either. And that's ok! Let's go back to the quote:

"If you are kind, people may accuse you of selfish, ulterior motives. Be kind anyway.

What you spend years building, someone could destroy overnight. Build anyway.

The good you do today, people will often forget tomorrow. Do good anyway.

Give the world the best you have, and it may never be enough. Give the world the best you've got anyway.

You see, in the final analysis, it is between you and your God … anyway."

What will it hurt if we love others anyway? The Shame Shadow© will tell you lies that it is a "risk, a gamble, they won't return it, you deserve the hurt, the abuse because you are *nothing*." But when we have grounded ourselves, we remember who we are. We are from deity. We are children of God. We stand to gain so much more than we could possibly lose—if we stay in the light and not in the dark.

I work with a lot of people who were in abusive relationships/ situations (physically, mentally, emotionally, spiritually, financially, verbally, etc.). Some want to continue to love, help, or fix, their abuser and "do good anyway." What do I tell them? The logic of still wanting to help someone who abused them seems very twisted, yet it happens (we won't go into the reasons why here).

I share with my clients that they can continue to help people who are in deep need if they want to but they must do so from a distance. This is what I teach them:

Imagine you are a lighthouse. Where are lighthouses found? Lighthouses are found on rock, high up if possible. They must be built on rock to be foundationally sound. They are not found in the ocean waves and water. Again, they are foundationally sound and are located in safe settings.

What is the purpose of a lighthouse? The purpose of a lighthouse is to warn ships of danger, like rocky shelves, coral reefs, etc., and to guide them to safe harbors. How do they do that? All lighthouses have a beacon of light that comes from them. The first types of lighthouses were towers with a woodfire built on top of them. The wooden fires were lit, and they helped to warn the ships of the dangers ahead. But, eventually, the use of candles and lamps were used. To amplify the light, mirrors were used. Mirrors set at different angles could increase the intensity of the light to about 400 times its candlepower.

If you are in abuse, you symbolically, are *not* a lighthouse yet. You are in a boat in the raging ocean. You cannot save anyone but yourself. Your job is to find a lighthouse, a pinpoint of light if you are in the darkest abyss, and follow that pinpoint until it leads you to another brighter one, until you see a beacon of light guiding you to a safe harbor, out of the raging storm. Remember, the water is trying to destroy you physically, spiritually, mentally, emotionally, verbally, financially etc. You will not be able to help anyone until you are out of danger yourself.

When you get out of your abusive situation *and find time to heal*, can you go back and help others? The answer is yes, but not in the way you think. You can help them as the lighthouse. You must remain at a safe distance. You can use your light to send a beacon of light out towards them through prayer, good wishes, and directing them to sound programs. You can pray that they will find programs that work with victims and abusers, etc. But you *cannot* directly help them. That is not your job.

Let's ask the question, if a lighthouse is NOT built on a strong foundation it cannot serve its purpose to help others out of danger. The same is true if you are not built on a firm foundation; you cannot become a beacon of light. Beacons warn of danger, beacons guide through the storms, and beacons bring you into safe harbor. That goes for wanting to help other victims to become victors as well. Bottomline, a huge piece of this healing is understanding that you must have light in order to be a beacon to someone else. You must find your light, fuel it, and then you can amplify your light to the world! We will talk specifically about these processes in the next 3 chapters.

Let's bring this full circle. I started the chapter with this quote: "Light, love, and lack: when we have light, we have love, therefore, we lack nothing. But, when we lack, we have neither light nor love." Do you see now why opposition in all things to make all things possible?

If we can make a choice to accept that, we are given the gift of peace. This is the Savior's ultimate gift—peace. Its power stops hate, anger, and madness. It is the true love that we feel. Instead of fighting off what we don't know, or don't want, maybe, just maybe we can accept what we lack as part of the "opposition in all things" and then exercise faith to take action. Our "trying in action" even with all our shortcomings is what will lead to love!

We can make the choice to be brave enough to enter Learning Zones more frequently and leave our Comfort Cage more and more. Even though we know that the Shame

Shadow© will strike. Plan on it. Get into the Learning Zone anyway. See what you can learn, and who you can become. In the end, it is between you and your God anyway. He will direct you to understand what it really means to love and forgive yourself, to love and forgive others, and how love is the driving force that makes life connected and possible.

SECTION 4

Finding, Fueling, and Amplifying Your Light

CHAPTER 12

Find your Light and Trim your Wick

An oil lamp becomes brighter after trimming, the truth becomes clearer when discussed. Many see light by lighting a lamp. When the truer light comes from within.—April Tribe Giauque

"Then spake Jesus again unto them, saying, I am the light of the world: he that followeth me shall not ʾwalk in darkness, but shall have the light of life. I am the Light of the World" (John 8:12)

Find your light! I want you to know that you all have light within you. You all have a spark and flame—a source of energy that lights up your eyes! It's called self-worth, self-love, and I say **LIGHT!** Where is it found and Who gave it to you? Your Creator, your Heavenly Father gave you this light. It is your soul. It helps to direct you to know right from wrong. Your light helps you learn how to make choices, act as a guide, and change how you see the world. It helps you to see light in the darkness.

Since you have life, you have light! I want you to know that you can brighten your light no matter what you have been through in this lifetime: abuse, abandonment, anger, hurt, pain, death, loss, sorrow, divorce, disappointment, shame, loss of perfection, failures at home, work, or school. ANYTHING!

Your light, your worth, your identity is something that you can *always increase* with love and action. As you surround yourself with others who have light, your light will also increase. Part of the success in surrounding yourself with more light is that you will begin to know who you are. Light will speak to others spirit-to-spirit and your identity will be revealed. It is crucial to know who you are, why you are here, and where you are going! That all comes back to LIGHT! Ready? Let's FIND your LIGHT!

Remember in chapter 2 we "geeked" out about the stars and what light is? We will geek out for a bit in this chapter too. Light. What is it? In nature, it is both a particle and a wave (well, some are still debating this, but for our purposes we will say that it is both). It's called a **Photon.**

- They have no electric charge.

- They are stable.

- They carry energy and momentum which are dependent on the frequency.

- They can have interactions with other particles such as electrons.

- They can be destroyed or created by many natural processes.

- When in empty space, they travel at the speed of light.

- They have zero mass.

Light is truly amazing to see all the differences it has and what it is. Depending on the type of matter it comes into contact with, light will behave differently. Sometimes light will pass directly through the matter, like with air or water. This type of matter is called transparent. Other objects completely reflect light, like an animal or a book. These objects are called opaque. A third type of object does some of both and tends to scatter the light. These objects are called translucent objects.

That is super amazing, and I feel even more evidence of a Creator—my Heavenly Father. As we have the very elements and light as the stars. Well, like everything we have learned thus far, there will be an opposite of light—darkness. For our purposes we have darkness called the Shame Shadow©.

We talked in chapter four about this darkness and in order to have that balance each one of us has it. Darkness knows our *weakness* and bam! He tries to get us. But we can get right back up because we are divinely created and filled with light! Remember it is a choice we have whether we are going to spend our time looking backward at the shadow that is cast behind us, or whether we are going to look ahead, fixed on the light in front of us? Let's do all - we can to stay fixed on the light and when mistakes happen, we can repent and be forgiven.

Let's look at another symbolism. Think about yourselves as an oil lamp. You are a vessel that holds oil, that has a wick to draw up the oil, and a flame that burns in order to cast your light. Without the wick your flame would burn sporadically and take up all the oil in a flash, leaving you burned out. In order to keep your light burning brightly you need to care for the wick and keep it trimmed. Trimming your wick and making it ready to receive the light is crucial to keeping it burning.

If you have ever noticed the wicks on some candles? Wicks can overburn meaning they clumped together forming a thick sooty part. Since we are burning each day, we need to trim our wick of the sooty blackened part. Those sooty parts are the negative thoughts from our shame, guilt, or all that we lack! If we are thinking we are a vessel of light, the flame should be at least the width of the wick, and even, not ragged. Once all the negative ragged part is cut off the wick will burn cleanly all the way up to the highest flame it can make. Giving you a shine and a light attacking positivity and love toward each other.

Light Illuminates and Darkness Disorients.

As you find that light and trim your wick, you'll brighten your life and push out more darkness, which is the difference between you and your dreams. We have to reach inside ourselves and find our light! We all have light, and as long as we have breath in our body, our light will *never* go out. Even standing in some of the darkest times in my life, my light never went out; and when I turned my light toward- others, the results were transformational.

One step at a time toward my light

I looked at the soft light of the night light as it kissed the faces of my five children that Christmas night. All were finally sleeping. We were away from abuse, from the fear, and we had a home. All were safe. All was well.

I turned and stepped into the hall. I placed one foot on the bottom step and worked my way upward. Free from abuse, step. Free from darkness, step. Free from fear, step. Strong in the light, step. I can do the hard things, step. My Heavenly Father never left me, step. All of us have shelter, step. We have food, step. I have my job, step. I am aware of the Shame Shadow©, step. When it tries to scream and be shrill, I don't feel my light go out, step. I found myself at the top of the landing and I smiled.

Seven of my nine years of marriage my first husband harbored lies, addiction, alcoholism, theft, fear, anxiety, physical blows, neglect, isolation, adultery, psychosis, mental illness, emotional abuse, and financial abuse. (The story is complex and can be found in my other book "Pinpoints of Light: Escaping the Abyss of Abuse" for all of those stories). In reflection of all of the darkness we had faced, to be basking in light on Christmas Eve was incredible.

I turned from the step toward the living room and looked again at the lights from the banister railing, the candles, and the string of lights from the Christmas tree. The light from all Christmas was shining gently and peacefully. I felt love sweep over me. I felt warm inside, and I could feel my light dance. I smiled a deep loving smile, standing in all of the different lights. We had overcome so much.

I found my feet carrying me toward those little pinpoints of light from the tree. I touched each gentle light bulb. Each one seemed to be a victory and my heart remembered more: free from anorexia, from child molestation, from abuse, from self-injury, from doubt, from poverty, from homelessness, from mental illness, from domestic violence, from fear, from shame.

I understood the shame and how it worked. I used it as a guide when I felt it. I acknowledge it and breathed through it.

My physical, emotional, and spiritual steps towards each pinpoint of light had been all choices I had to make. They were all decisions. We have a choice in how we will react or respond to everything. I quietly stepped back from the tree and looked at the splendor of each pinpoint and all that it meant to me. And now, I could truly say, all was well!

If you could have shown me this scene a year earlier, I would have had a hard time believing you because I was in such a dark abyss of abuse.

Mental, emotional, and physical abuse can dim light. The night my ex-husband attacked us, strangled me, pointed the gun at us and himself, we didn't know if the light of day would return. But, it did. We were drawn to pinpoints of light scattered along our path in order to climb our way out. When I was actively seeking for more light, I was faithful in the "trimming of my wick." I was getting rid of the darkness and negativity that the Shame Shadow© constantly was whispering to me and turning from looking at the shadow to looking into the light.

Find your Light and Trim your wick:

READY? Let's do this! Action items are important; they get us to move. At the end of this chapter I have provided a space for you to write in if you wish or you can write it someplace else. Let's be bold! Ready? Write down how your light feels and why it is important to you.

I believe in you! Just think, what you are writing may inspire someone else—your light will amplify theirs!

How your light feels and why it is important to you.

CHAPTER 13

Fuel Your Light

If you fuel your journey on the opinions of others, you are going to run out of gas—April Tribe Giauque

Angels speak by the power of the Holy Ghost; wherefore, they speak the words of Christ. Wherefore, I said unto you, feast upon the words of Christ; for behold, the words of Christ will tell you all things what ye should do.—2 Nephi 32: 3

We know all about the Shame Shadow©, the Learning Zone, and the Comfort Cage. We know how to Ground ourselves, and all about Hecklers. We also know about the Vulnerability Prism, and the long and short of the Recovery Road. We understand where our light came from, so now we need to keep our light fueled.

In order for us to keep the light burning brighter, we *must* keep oil in our lamps. What is the oil? It is the positivity that fuels our light. But how do we find the fuel for it? Here are three ways: physically, mentally, and spiritually.

Physically

How do I fuel my lamp physically? We need to move our body somehow in order to connect and fuel it. What helps you to add oil to your lamp physically? Listen to your body. Go for a walk, a run, swim, spin, lift, do some yoga? I'd love for you to make a list of what you need to do physically to connect and add the drops of positive light to your lamp.

Morning Light

Left over right, bunny ear tight, then around over and through and now I've tied my shoe. I can't help it. Every time I tie my shoe, I say that in rhythm. I stand and look out the blackened window telling myself that it is still o-dark-hundred, but I must get out and run/walk my three miles otherwise I can't seem to set the rest of my day. I really need movement to center me.

I grasp hold of the handle twist it quietly and step out into the muggy summer Austin morning. At 4:30 am it's a sticky-sticky morning at 83 degrees with 80% humidity. It feels like a steam room on this July morning. I reach out for the railing and start some of my stretches. Mornings are stiff, but like the Tinman, I loosen up finally. One final stretch and then the familiar pattern of left and right as my feet start pumping me up the street.

As my legs carry me, my mind wanders into a type of prayer. I give in to the rhythm and open my mind to the gift of God, listening in the quiet of the morning for thoughts, promptings/nudges, and sometimes answers.

With each mile underneath my shoes, I am closer to filling my oil lamp with the energy and fuel I'll need to take on the day with a family of 11. This physical energy is a saving grace when I have to pull 19-20-hour days. One day, that will calm down, but for now my saving grace is running. I rounded the corner and whisper a moment of thanks as more answers are found. This run has set me straight and I feel ready to take on the rush of the day.

Please list what you do physically

❧

Mentally

Next step: how do I fuel my lamp mentally? By mentally I also mean intellectually. Your brain does a lot of thinking and you need to be able to fill it with as much positivity as possible to combat the Shame Shadow©. We have to feed it and care for it. What helps you add oil to your lamp mentally, to drawn on and brighten your light? Do you invest in the time yourself?

Mental Garden

Plastic grocery sack, check! Weed trowel, check! Garden gloves, check! Headphones and latest podcast download, check! YES! Bring it on, Texas size weeds! *You don't stand a one-hour chance with me!* I say in my head, "I'll get you my little pretties and your little dog too!" No weed stands a chance If I am armed up with such battle gear. It is awesome!

The sharp metal cuts through the earth. With my strain on the blade as I pull back, I hear the snapping of the deep roots. I begin to wiggle it back and forth snapping more and more roots and with my gloved hand, I grasp the base of the weed and start to pull. With a sickening sound like a tooth being pulled from a giant, the weed releases, and I put in the bag.

Suddenly through my ears come words that lead my mind into another world. I can feel the joy and the euphoria of being lost in a great story. There is nothing better! My mind flows to the audiobook as I listen to the truth resonating in my ears and my heart. My hands and arms go into autopilot, pulling the weeds as my mind is fed on the rich food of the story.

After an hour and true to form, I fill 14 grocery bags full of weeds. AHHH springtime in Texas! As I continue to pull the weed and feed my mind in this manner, it is powerful! I can remember more because my body is moving and active. My little synapses in my brain are firing and I am holding onto the information. I almost feel the droplets of oil filling into my mind, giving me a sense of growth. I feel a bit of a euphoric feeling and can't wait to learn more. Suddenly I look around me and the sack of weeds are overflowing, and the yard looks amazing. My mind is well fed, and my yard looks great. Totally a two for one activity.

Please list what you do mentally

Spiritually

Finally, how do I fill my lamp spiritually? For me, I must immerse myself in scriptures, good talks, going to church, visiting and ministering to friends and neighbors, and in good, spiritual music! These are the keys to my success. What brightens your light spiritually? Do you feast on the Word? Pray? Meditate? Time for pondering? Time for journaling? Good connecting music?

Commuting to Christ

6:42 am. I fire up the engine of my car, turn on the headlights to slice a pathway in the dark morning. I check the rearview mirror one last time. I see both my deaf girls in the back seat immersed in their books as I back out of the driveway. It is time for the "great Austin traffic commute." We only live 18 miles from the school and work but it's a solid one-hour drive.

As my wheels roll along the interstate, It's time for the good word of God. I hit play on my smartphone and the car comes alive with light. I find myself on the road to Jericho walking with the Savior. I can see His face and I begin to wonder how I would respond with the questions he is asking. I also think about the woman at the well. What was she thinking? I love to feel the Spirit guide me as I seek this truth.

As the miles creep underneath, me, I have a great amount of time to ponder and to reflect on what I hear from the scriptures. I speak notes into my phone to mark down my thoughts. I glance at the rear-view mirror and two heads are so bent over their books that they don't even see me. I focus forward and back into the word. There is more time to feed my spirit. This powerful work fuels my lamp with oil—deep rich oil that gives my soul what it craves each morning and sets my day in line with my values and my conviction.

I love the way the oil flows into the lamp for an hour each morning. Who knew that a crazy commute could lead me to this powerful time with my Heavenly Father, learning His will for me? This is true scorching power against the Shame Shadow©.

Spiritually: What do you do to fill your lamp?

Please List what you do Spiritually

CHAPTER 14

Amplify Your Light!

Generally speaking, the most miserable people I know are those who are obsessed with themselves; the happiest people I know are those who lose themselves in the service of others... By and large, I have come to see that if we complain about life, it is because we are thinking only of ourselves.—Gordon B. Hinckley

"And behold, I tell you these things that ye may learn wisdom; that ye may learn that when ye are in the service of your fellow beings ye are only in the service of your God" (Mosiah 2:17)

In one of my favorite books, a wise teacher asks if we "should light a candle and then hide it under a bushel? Or should we hold it up for all to see?" What good is hiding a light?

Aren't we using light as a means of how to see things in the dark? Here are a few questions to ask yourself: Do you let your light shine? Do you shine for many, or for just a few? Are you afraid to shine? If we are afraid shine our light, we might be holding the Vulnerability Prism. And as we hold that all of weakness are exposed. However, holding it is the only way to show the courage. With that courage we try different things—even if we are afraid!

We have all felt that feeling of being exposed and vulnerable to something. When that happens, we have a choice to put ourselves out on the line. When we are putting our "light" on the line, it makes us vulnerable. Can you name a time when you were the most vulnerable? Can you describe what happened? Did you think you were going to survive it? At the time I bet you thought that you were NOT going to survive it, but look! You did! You are here, and you just read through those questions. You have already made it through your worst day.

In chapter twelve and thirteen you learned about how to fuel your light. Now we are on a mission to help you amplify your light. The questions that were posed to you about holding your candle up and shining your light are important questions to ask yourself because you will need to know how ready you are to let your light shine out toward others. One final question, how do you amplify light?

Let's geek out for a bit. Like we learned in the last chapter, light is both a particle and a wave. That means it can be reflected and be amplified. How? Light is reflected and the wave is intensified with mirrors, prisms, and lenses to amplify the wave. The wave is stretched and yet the light does not thin—it maintains the brightness and is in fact amplified. Lighthouses use this method to shoot the light of an oil lamp to beam up to 20 miles! That is true power.

Think about the light you have inside of you. Think about how you can fuel it. Now think about how you can amplify your light like a lighthouse, using lenses and mirrors to reflect and concentrate the light. The way that we amplify your light is through action. The action is called service. Can you amplify your light through service? Yes, you do it all the time. Think about your service like lenses and mirrors reflecting light. Write down what those acts of service are and how they amplify your outreach to anyone with whom you interact.

How far of a reach does your light have? Great question, right? Think about a house. Let's say, symbolically, that your light without mirrors or lenses can light up one room in the house. Does it help others? Yes. For anyone who needs light in that room, they will be able to feel it and it will help them to turn away from their shadows of darkness. It might only be enough for one person, but that is great! If that is who you can help at the time, then it is right!

Now, think if you added a mirror to your light through your acts of service. Do you think you could light up the whole house? Sure! Finally, what if, through service, you added a few more mirrors and lenses to your light? Could your light symbolically reach beyond the house in a concentrated beam to those who were 20 miles away? Daily service is like the mirrors and lenses that can reach more people, even someone who is far away.

The goal of this chapter is to make you aware of your light. And to find out if there are times when you are only able to light up one room, a whole house, or beam outside of the house through the storms of life to help others out in the deep. Asking questions like does my light fill one room or can I reach others, is a balance to know where you are at and if you can do more. If you want to shine in just one room of your life for now, that's fine. Let's start where you are!

Snow Service

Some of my early mornings were filled with quiet, cold, and muffled silence because that was the sound of snow. As snow-flakes fell and began to stack on top of one another, piling higher and higher, there was excitement in the air.

I threw on my winter coat, boots, gloves, a hat, and snuck out the side door. I popped into the garage, grabbed Big Blue, the snow shovel, and trudged through the snowbank, meeting my father on the other side. He never looked up from his work but started whistling once he saw me.

As a child about six or seven, I would watch my dad get up early in the morning, go through the garage, walk around to side gate and tromp through the snow to the back shed. He would unlock the door and flip on the light of the shed. That light would cast a small echo of light that would spill across the ceiling of my room because my window faced the west—I could look out into our backyard, and that was where I would find my dad in the light of the shed, firing up the John Deere snow blower.

Once the snow machine was thundering and turning over, my dad would engage the blade and the yellow and green machine would dig into the snow, eating a pathway through the white blanket of my backyard toward the front gate, through the gate and then in a side-to-side pattern, throwing the snow off the driveway and onto the side. The power and hum of that machine was my clue to quickly pull on my winter gear and head outside with the blue shovel to meet up with my dad.

Sometimes the hum of the snowplow didn't wake me, but the slide scrape, slide scrape, slide scrape of the shovel would. Repeating again and again. Rhythmic and patterned and predictable. I looked out the side window that faced my neighbor's yard. My breath fogged up the cold glass and

I wiped it down again. Through the dark morning, I saw a black silhouette moving snow. It was my dad.

Together we worked to clear the snow from two more driveways. It was hard work, but there was a feeling in my eight-year-old heart that I was warm, filled with light and power. I remember as I shook off my boots and removed my sweat and snow-heavy coat that this was different than a fun time, this was a deeper feeling. Serving others, helping someone with the skills and talents that you have is a powerful feeling of light and love.

When I was eight and helped my dad, I didn't know what to call this feeling. One time during a snow day, I asked my dad what I was feeling. He said, "That's the feeling of snow service. It warms you every time." From that day until now, each time the sky darkens, and the temperature drops I get a rush of excitement for snow and the anticipation of the "snow service" feeling. I'm proud to say, it still happens today.

Why would service infect my heart like that? Let's look at the quote again from Gordon B Hinckley,

"Generally speaking, the most miserable people I know are those who are obsessed with themselves; the happiest people I know are those who lose themselves in the service of others... By and large, I have come to see that if we complain about life, it is because we are thinking only of ourselves."

The happiest people are those that lose themselves in the service of others. Again, in one of my favorite books, a wise master taught that if we love our neighbor as ourselves, we would be blessed with light and love. That is another way to think about service. True service means that your heart is seeking to help someone else. But I will say, if you start out your service in a begrudging manner, thinking about all the stuff you have to do, but help anyway, it doesn't take long for that attitude to drop away as you see what the service is doing for the other person and for your own heart. That is the power of amplifying your light.

The question is, where will you shine today: in one room, the house, or as a beam from a lighthouse?

Shine in one room: Deep breathe with eyes closed. Look inside and see that light gentle in your heart. Now, trim your wick and gently dip the wick to that light. Watch the dark—the lack of light lick the wick and shine for your room. Invite one or two others to come in and feel of the heat and maybe even read by that light. Share a story, share a text with someone! Work at your own pace but please, share!

Shine the house: Now that you have shared in one room and those three people, do you see that the light is brighter? Let's share in the great room with that light. Then we can light the whole the kitchen, dining room, and living room. Isn't the brightness of this powerful!?

Shine as a BEACON of LIGHT for all to see: It's time to step out and really shine! Become the Beacon of Light by shining and amplifying your light as from a lighthouse. You are amplifying your light by reflecting it.

Based on your feelings today, where are you able to serve someone else? Did you shine in one room? Did you shine in a house? Or did you shine outside for all the see? Remember that the point of amplifying your light is to serve someone.

—WARNING— this is not a competition about who can outshine someone. Think about chapter four and the Shame Shadow© and how the poison of the three P's: *pleasing, perfecting, and performing* can be extremely damaging. If we start to compete or compare our service to to someone else's then we have lost the point of what amplifying our light means. Remember, nothing is perfect, but there is perfection in practicing your service. Action is the practice of perfection. Nothing is perfect but there is perfection in practicing your action.

Please brainstorm some ideas of what you will do if you shine in one room, the whole house, or as a beacon of light from a lighthouse?

One Room	Whole house	Beacon of Light

CHAPTER 15

Out of Darkness

Owning our story can be hard but not nearly as difficult as spending our lives running from it. Embracing our vulnerabilities is risky but not nearly as dangerous as giving up on love and belonging and joy—the experiences that make us the most vulnerable. Only when we are brave enough to explore the darkness will we discover the infinite power of our light. —Brene Brown

"Therefore, hold up your light that it may shine unto the world. Behold I am the light which ye shall hold up—that which ye have seen me do. Behold ye see that I have prayed unto the Father, and ye all have witnessed." (3 Nephi 18:24).

Light, love and lack—this was going to be the title of this book, but I ended up tweaking is just a bit to find so that action could be taken in a direction towards more light. You see, we started this journey together with chapter one talking about how there is opposition in all things: light and darkness, health and sickness, joy and sorrow, what we have and what we lack etc. The point was to establish a very important truth that we can't *eliminate* the opposition, but that with opposition, agency or making choices becomes possible.

We all have the agency to choose how to respond to what happens during this life. We don't have control of *what* happens in this life, but we do have control of our *responses* to it. This is a hard lesson to learn for people who are stuck in "pleasing, performing, and perfecting." People who are stuck in the three p's feel that they can control life so that only the good happens. But if we are trying to control and force things, we are no better than the destroyer who tries to force people into making poor choices.

The destroyer will set traps and snares, lie, and tell half-truths to keep us bound to him as he gently leads us down to our destruction. We must be vigilant to keep cutting away the destroyer's flaxen cords that he tries to bind us with. We must keep cutting them away through repentance and turning toward the light. With the opposition, we are able to make choices and through those decisions we can choose light or everything that we lack, which lies in the darkness. Lack really refers to the Shame Shadow©— that voice that tries to fill us with doubt with all that we *lack*. The circumstances might be out of our control but our choice in how we respond or react is ours to make. "Doubt your doubts before you doubt your faith." (Dieter F. Uchtdorf).

How many times in life have you felt like you were on the Recovery Road just resting and enjoying the moment when suddenly there was a phone call with life changing news, a car accident, natural disaster, or job loss and you are thrust into the Learning Zone thinking, I'm not yet ready to be back here, but nonetheless, there you are. It takes a few minutes, hours or days to switch gears, accept that that is where you are and get ready to learn. The Shame Shadow© is right there ready to extend the darkness toward you whether you are ready or not. It can be messy at first in the Learning Zone and you might even be running for that Comfort Cage to "regroup." I know I've run from my faith many times back to the Comfort Cage depending on the circumstances—and that's ok!

My point in writing this book is for you to recognize your patterns: your fears your tendencies, your vulnerabilities, your grounding techniques, and how to recognize the sound of hecklers. It is also to understand that we if we stay in our Comfort Cage, we have damned our progress in learning and eventually there will be a catalyst that forces us to leave and start learning and growing. We also need to remember that **we** have the power to turn away from the Shame Shadow© and choose light.

In giving the circumstances of life these different labels and names, the power in labeling something is to help you to recognize it as it happened or very soon afterward so that you can use your agency to make a choice—light or darkness. That is the empowerment of agency. It is beautiful and frustrating all at the same time. But one thing is for sure, our agency to choose is for all of us here on earth. Wisdom teaches us that we must take advantage despite our circumstances that we have *the* choice in how we respond or react.

If you are reading that and start to ask questions like, but what about people who are born in other countries, born with war and civil unrest raging all around them, or people who are in abuse? We might think, *That's not right, that's not fair. What choice do they have?* They have the same as you. They can learn how to respond to it all through the agency they have been given by our creator.

Will they fight off what they lack and turn toward what they have? Will they step into the Learning Zone and out of the Comfort Cage? Will they ignore the Hecklers? Will they hold the Vulnerability Prism? Will they learn how to ground themselves? Will they reflect and recover on the Recovery Road? Will they ultimately turn from the darkness of the Shame Shadow© by not listening to it, and by not allowing it to have power over them? Yes. We all have the same agency to make these choices no matter our circumstances.

Remember in chapter 11 about the love we can feel and give in this life. We know that we must have love in order to live, and when we don't receive love, we spend a lifetime trying to find it, or a lifetime of running from the pain of that loss. Love is a true power that brings life to life. We all know when we experience a loss of love—it is so painful, and we know when we have experienced the deepest love—it is the ultimate joy! Love is what we are seeking when we look toward the Light of all Light. Light can fill us with such love, and it helps us to combat and fight off the pain that happens in our lives.

Remember we have the choice to respond to our circumstances like this:

"If you are kind, people may accuse you of selfish, ulterior motives. *Be kind anyway.*
What you spend years building, someone could destroy overnight. *Build anyway.*
The good you do today, people will often forget tomorrow. *Do good anyway.*
Give the world the best you have, and it may never be enough. *Give the world the best you've got anyway.* You see, in the final analysis, it is *between you and your God ... anyway.*"—Mother Teresa

In looking at that quote through the mindset of coming *Out of Darkness* and becoming a beacon of light it could read:

If you shine your light toward others and they try to dim it with negativity and darkness— *shine anyway*. Others will still see it.

As you are fueling your lamp through physical, mental, and spiritual means and others try to take and take and syphon your energy—*fuel anyway*.

When you do good, help others, see the need and fill it through your actions while others mock, belittle, or take advantage of you—give them the benefit of the doubt and *amplify your light though serving others anyway*!

In the end, you only have one life to live, so fulfill your calling with that life *through your light anyway*. In the end it is between you and your God—anyway.

Remember what we lack is not who we are. What we lack can be gained through, faith, prayers, and action. That's the opportunity the Learning Zone gives to us. When we learn that our lack is not a hindrance or a weakness, but it is given to us so that we can find our strengths, we gain real power! It takes a mindset shift to understand that and to be the power God wants us to be. But we can do it!

And who does He want us to be? He wants us to come *Out of Darkness* and become a Beacon of Light to the family of God. When we are that light, we are able to help, guide, and bring others back to safety through our light and actions. As we shine with truth and with light, we are able to bring people love. True love of God is never-ending and so fulfilling that we will never thirst or hunger again.

As we shine with the amplification of serving others, our outreach can help people. We may not even know of or understand who is watching us. So many of our brothers and sisters can be given a guide and direction home toward Him if we do our part: shine our light, keep it fueled, and amplify it to all.

Why do we do this? We want to help our brothers and sisters know the way Home. All have their agency and will choose to follow or leave. They may get lost for a time, but then remember to search for answers, and turn away from the darkness and shadow to find the light. This light might be as small as a pinpoint because of how far they have drifted away. However, as they follow it, they are gaining more and more light toward the Beacon of Light—which leads our brothers and sisters back to our Heavenly family home.

I'll leave you with this final thought.

Start where you are at in this journey to come *Out of Darkness.*

Take things hour by hour, day by day, or month to month if you have to.

Celebrate your wins.

Take time to cry.

And know, you are NEVER alone in this journey. I'm with you, the Lord is with you, and you are with you. Trust you to live in your Light! You are Worth It!

OUT OF DARKNESS TO BECOME A
BEACON OF LIGHT

LIGHT SHINE

There is a saying from my favorite book that says, "Let your Light so Shine!" Many times, over the years, I felt that light was so far away from me. I was in an abyss of abuse. I was lost in heavy tangible darkness. How could I ever find my light again become a light to others? It was such a dark time.

Suddenly, *Pinpoints of Light* were cast before me in that dark abyss. I inched my way towards them. I could feel a gentle heat and warmth begin in my chest. It was as if I imagined me rising from my tangled darkened soul towards the light! That energy began to sooth, enrich, and enlighten me. I was stepping *Out of Darkness* leaving the cold bleakness behind!

How? What did I do?

Welcome to LIGHT SHINE!

Light Shine is the companion course of my book *Out of Darkness*. I take you on a deeper dive of how to overcome pain, fear, and shame that thrive in darkness and break down the book into a 10-week coaching course to help you find your pathway to healing.

This program I walk with you and help you face the dark places that you have been stuck or trapped in. You have a choice to get out! If you have been hiding in a Comfort Cage, I'll help you come out and into the Learning Zone. After reading the book, I can empathize with you. I know how this dark place happens. I have been there as well.

The question is, how many of you are ready to step *out of the darkness* and into the light?

- Imagine finding your individual worth and shining that worth for others to see.

- Imagine the journey of healing from the deep darkness of pain, fear, or shame into the dawn of life by learning your self-worth, your strength, your value, and your power!

- Imagine how to share your light, your power, and your love with others who are broken to add more light to them and to help them cast out darkness and fear!

Are you ready? Let' help you "let your light so shine!"
Go to www.lightshinecourse.com and begin your journey to healing today. I'll be right there to guide you. If you would like more information, email me at april@apriltribe.com or visit my website www.apriltribegiauque.com

LIGHT SHINE

L   LIGHT: THE NEVER-ENDING POWER

I   INVITATION TO LEARNING ZONE

G   GET TO KNOW THE ENEMY--THE SHAME SHADOW©

H   HEART OF THE COMFORT CAGE

T   THE SKILL OF GROUNDING

S   SOUL EXPOSURE: WHAT THE VULNERABILITY PRISM IS FOR

H   HEALING: WALKING YOUR RECOVERY ROAD

I   INTERNAL WORK: FINDING YOUR LIGHT

N   NEVER EMPTY: HOW TO FUEL YOUR LIGHT

E   ENERGY: HOW TO AMPLIFY YOUR LIGHT THROUGH SERVICE.

OUT OF DARKNESS

WWW.APRILTRIBEGIAUQUE.COM

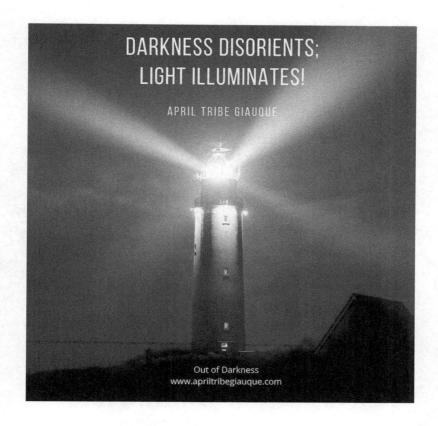

MANY SEEK LIGHT BY LIGHTING A
LAMP WHEN THE TRUER LIGHT COMES
FROM WITHIN.

APRIL TRIBE GIAUQUE

Notes

Introduction:

1. Churchill, Winston. "Never Give In." nationalchurchillmuseum. org. 29, October, 1941.www. https://www.national churchillmuseum.org/never-give-in-never-never-never.html

Opposition in All Things

1. Marden, Orin Sweet. "Success is not measured." https:// izquotes.com/quote/orison-swett-marden/success-is-not-measured-by-what-you-accomplish-but-by-the-opposition-you-have-encountered-and-the-119615

2. The Family: A Proclamation to the World," *Ensign,* Nov. 2010, 129

3. Holland. Jeffery. R. "We are All Enlisted," General Conference. Oct 2011.23

Let There Be Light

1. Baker, Ella. *"Give Light and People will Find a Way."* https://southinblackandwhite.files.wordpress.com/2012/01/givelight-peoplefindway-tyson.pdf

2. Howell, Elizabeth. "Humans Really Are Made Out of Star Dust." Space.com. https://www.space.com/35276-humans-made-of-stardust-galaxy-life-elements.html

Learning Zone

1. Walstein, Howard. *"Do Something Uncomfortable Today."* https://www.google.com/search?sxsrf=ACYBGNSPU3Kao33lcEJWDYwUgFFX1ydBug:1578239237215&q=Where+do+I+find+Walstein,+Howard.+%E2%80%9CDo+Something+Uncomfortable+Today.%E2%80%9D&tbm=isch&source=univ&sa=X&ved=2ahUKEwiU9-qo5-zmAhUYX80KHSGZB9MQ7Al6BAgIECQ&biw=1315&bih=674#imgrc=xcPzArEIISqn4M:

Shame Shadow©

1. Grace. "You cannot stand in the Light While Sheltering in the Darkness." Coolnsmart.com 1, January, 2013. https://www.coolnsmart.com/darkness_quotes/

Fallen Angel

1. Jung, Carl. "I am not what happened to me" https://en.wikiquote.org/wiki/Talk:Carl_Jung